PUB WALKS

— I

County I
and Teesside

Charlie Emett

COUNTRYSIDE BOOKS
NEWBURY, BERKSHIRE

First published 2005

COUNTRYSIDE BOOKS
3 Catherine Road
Newbury, Berkshire

To view our complete range of books,
please visit us at
www.countrysidebooks.co.uk

ISBN 1 85306 912 4

*For my dear friends
Bill and Ron
We still walk the fields together.*

Photographs and maps by Ron Dodsworth

Produced through MRM Associates Ltd., Reading
Typeset by Techniset Typesetters, Newton-le-Willows
Printed by Arrowsmith, Bristol

Contents

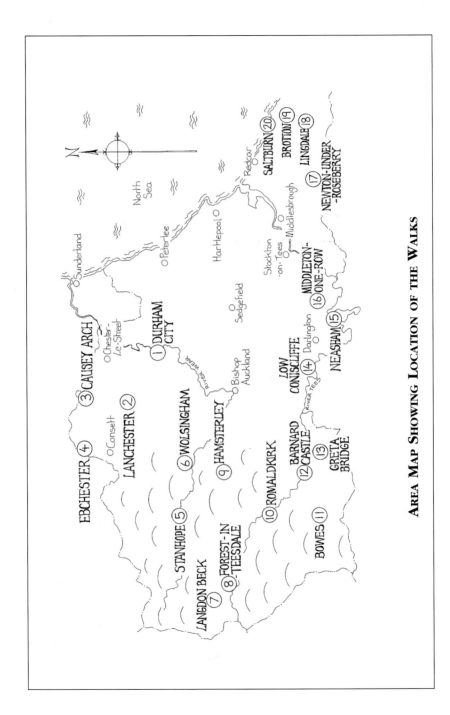

AREA MAP SHOWING LOCATION OF THE WALKS

Walk

PUBLISHER'S NOTE

We hope that you obtain considerable enjoyment from this book; great care has been taken in its preparation. However, changes of landlord and actual closures are sadly not uncommon. Likewise, although at the time of publication all routes followed public rights of way or permitted paths, diversion orders can be made and permissions withdrawn.

We cannot, of course, be held responsible for such diversion orders and any inaccuracies in the text which might result from these or any other changes to the routes nor any damage which might result from walkers trespassing on private property. We are anxious though that all details covering the walks are kept up to date and would welcome information from readers which would be relevant to future editions.

The sketch maps accompanying each walk are intended to guide you to the starting point and give a simple but accurate idea of the route to be taken. For those who like the benefit of detailed maps, we recommend that you arm yourself with the relevant Ordnance Survey map.

INTRODUCTION

County Durham and adjacent Teesside lie at the very heart of North East England, cradled between the glorious High Pennines westwards and the restless North Sea to the east. Together they cover more than 1,000 square miles between the highly populated areas of Newcastle and Gateshead to the north and Billingham and Middlesbrough to the south. Another conurbation gathers around Wearmouth, otherwise the whole area is essentially rural.

Three major rivers and their tributaries flow into this region, and they all rise in the Pennines. The Derwent follows County Durham's northern border through upland, woodland and farmland, eventually to join the Tyne. The Wear rises a little further west, on higher ground, and follows a tortuous course eastwards before turning north to curl around Durham Cathedral in a deep gorge. It continues its northern meander, then turns east, following a more direct route to the North Sea. The Tees has its genesis just below the rim of Cross Fell where the Pennines are at their highest. While still in impetuous infancy it tumbles down Cauldron Snout as a foaming cataract and plunges over the impressive falls of High and Low Force, continuing in a most delightful way through a patchwork of meadows, pastures and mixed woodland dotted with farms and cottages.

All the Durham dales lie in an Area of Outstanding Natural Beauty and all have reservoirs set high in their valleys like cerulean gems. From north to south there are five of them – Derwent, Tunstall, Burnhope, Selset and Baldersdale.

Flint and stone arrow heads found between the rivers Tyne and Tees indicate Stone Age Man living there as early as 8,000 years BC. Around 2,000 BC a new breed of man, who used tools and weapons of bronze, settled in the area and began clearing the forests. By about 700 BC Iron Age man had arrived. With the growing use of iron tools and weapons, the population spread. These people, who lived between the rivers Tyne and Tees belonged to the largest Celtic group of people in Iron Age Britain, the Brigantes. They controlled all the land between the Tyne and the Humber.

Following the Roman invasion of Britain in AD 43, the Brigantes resisted until around AD 78, when they succumbed to the Romans. Under the 350 years or so of Roman occupation, the Brigantes continued to farm as they always had – the Romans never introduced their own agricultural methods into what, to them, was merely a frontier district of the Roman Empire. Yet much evidence of Roman occupation remains in the form of roads, like Dere Street, place names, the remains of aqueducts, bath houses, central heating and collections of ornaments and coins.

When the Romans departed, Angles and Saxons from Denmark and northern Germany settled along the Northumberland coast and the land between the rivers Tyne and Tees became waste where, according to Simeon of Durham, 'it was nothing but a hiding place for wild and woodland beasts'.

During the 7th and 8th centuries, Christian 'English' became established in places like Darlington, Wolsingham and Cleatlam and gradually the pagan Angles and Saxons were converted to Christianity.

From these beginnings County Durham evolved to become a major supplier of coal, which has been mined there since medieval times. During the 1820s coal output dramatically increased as the East Durham coal field was developed. By 1911, almost 10% of the county's workforce, some 152,000 people, were coal miners and, by 1913, England's northern coalfield, 70% of which was in County Durham, produced 58.7 million tons of coal, a quarter of the national total. These coal fields have all gone now and the countryside has reverted to its former rural beauty. Hikers, who once took a chance with County Durham and Teesside, presuming the walks to be mediocre, have discovered the place, and return again and again, in ever increasing numbers, enchanted by the pleasuring reality of the walks!

These 20 short pub walks have been chosen as an introduction to County Durham and Teesside. Between them they contain everything for the country lover – a landscape comprising some of England's most impressive views, a rich variety of wildlife and a proliferation of folklore and history. The natives are friendly and the publicans are well used to satisfying the inner man or woman.

All the walks were chosen with the family in mind, none is too strenuous for anyone of moderate fitness and the routes are unambiguous and easy to follow. The average length of three miles places no great burden on even the inexperienced walker. In fact the walking is so satisfying and interest-filled that often the hiker finds that the walk ends too soon. This is where the pub from which the walk began comes into its own as any disappointment is soothed by the tempting fare offered inside.

OS Landranger maps have a scale of $1^1/_4$ inches to 1 mile and are adequate for all these walks. OS Explorer and Outdoor Leisure maps have a larger scale, $2^1/_2$ inches to 1 mile and show more detail. It is always advisable to supplement the sketch map with the relevant OS map.

The purpose of this book is to guide adventurous, country loving enthusiasts through pleasant parts of the 'Land of the Prince Bishops' in safety and to introduce them to some pleasant watering holes where they can savour the nectar and ambrosia on offer.

Slainte dhuitse, (health to you), and good walking.

Charlie Emett

Durham City
The Royal County Hotel

Durham's cathedral, castle and monastery have been declared one of the UK's first World Heritage Sites, ranking in importance alongside the Palace of Versailles and the Taj Mahal. Durham Cathedral is the jewel in the county's crown.

Durham's Norman cathedral and castle dominate the sandstone peninsula on which they stand, towering above the steep, wooded bend of the Wear which almost encloses them like a moat. Together cathedral and castle form the centre piece of Durham, the most visually exciting city in Britain.

The Royal County Hotel is sited close to the outer bank of the Wear as it curls around the peninsula, east of the castle, near Elvet Bridge. Built in 1630, it was formerly two houses. Lady Mary Radcliffe, whose half sister, Lady Mary Tudor, was the natural daughter of Charles II, lived in one; Elizabeth Bowes, aunt of Lord Strathmore's wife, Mary Eleanor Bowes, lived in the other. In compliance with her father's will, when Mary married, her husband was to take her family name, so John Lyon, Earl of Strathmore, assumed the name of Bowes. From the joining of these families was to come Elizabeth, our late Queen Mother. In the mid-19th century the houses were incorporated into a hotel, originally called the Dunelm. There is a carved black oak staircase in the hotel that is even older than the original building. It was salvaged from ruined Loch Leven Castle in Scotland, where Mary Queen of Scots, was a prisoner.

As a residence, before it became a hotel, famous personages stayed here. Cromwell did in 1650, on his way to the battle of Dunbar. Charles I hid there before his arrest for treason. More recently, Edward VII was a guest and it was then that the dignity of 'Royal' was added to the 'County'. Annually, on the third Saturday of July until recently, when most of Durham's coalfields were closed, leading Labour politicians would appear on the hotel balcony to view the proceedings at the Durham Miners' Gala.

As the hotel has expanded, every effort has been made to ensure that the old and the new have blended comfortably. It is opulent, smoothly efficient and exudes bonhomie. In the County Restaurant an exceptionally high quality menu includes such gastronomic delights as saddle of lamb sliced onto a potato rosti covered in a rich rosemary juice. The restaurant serves lunch daily between 12 noon and 2.30 pm and dinner from 7.30 pm to 10.15 pm (9.30 pm on Sunday). The brasserie, open all day, has a wide range of hot and cold food for lunch and dinner and the chef will happily advise on the day's display. Pastas include tagliatelle, garganelli and penne, each with a choice of sauces, and vegetarian dishes include quorn tikka masala with saffron rice. The Vaux-linked bar offers a hand-pulled Wards Best Bitter while Lorimer's Scotch and Samson beers and Labatt's and Heineken lagers are on draught.

Telephone: 01913 866821

● **HOW TO GET THERE:** Approaching Durham from the south, along the A167, turn right at the Cock O' the North, along the A1050. On reaching a roundabout, keep straight ahead along Church Street, which meets New Elvet at a tangent. Continue along it to a junction with Old Elvet. The Royal County Hotel is on the right hand corner.

● **PARKING:** There is a very large car park at the rear of the hotel, entered through an archway.

● **LENGTH OF THE WALK:** 2^1/$_2$ miles. Map: OS Explorer 308 (GR 277424).

THE WALK

(1) From the hotel entrance in Old Elvet, turn right and cross the facing road, New Elvet, continuing over the Wear on Elvet Bridge, the original of which was built by Bishop Puiset (1153–95). Immediately turn right, descend steps and turn right along a riverside path, going under the bridge and along Fearon Walk, still alongside the river. Hereabouts, the river is edged with Himalayan balsam, its blue flowers on six feet tall stems.

(2) Immediately after going under Kingsgate Bridge, turn right, up steps. At their top turn right onto Bow Lane and immediately turn left along it, passing on the right St Mary-le-Bow, once a church and now a magnificent museum. From the lane end, turn right, briefly, then turn left along Dun Cow Lane. This leads to the cathedral car park which edges Durham Cathedral on the left. Continue alongside the car park and, on reaching a path on the left which leads to a cathedral door with a splendid sanctuary knocker, take this detour which goes into the greatest Norman church in England.

Begun in 1093, Durham Cathedral was completed in 1133. The Galilee Chapel, (c1130) the Chapel of Nine Altars, (c1242), and the central tower, (c1490), are later additions.

Returning from the detour, turn left and continue alongside the cathedral, continuing past it to go between buildings along Windy Gap. At a junction of paths turn left along a broad path. On reaching steps on the right marked 'Archaeological Museum', turn right down them. Where the steps end, continue along a gently descending path. On reaching more steps, descend them and continue to meet another path at a tangent, which you follow, ignoring descending steps on the right.

The large building on your right is the archaeological museum, once a fulling mill.

(3) Stay on the path, passing Prebend's Bridge and keep edging the river. Soon a small folly is passed on the left. It stands near to where the Polish dwarf Count Barrowlaski was reputed to have lived. In fact, he lived in another part of Durham with his wealthy wife.

(4) On reaching Kingsgate Bridge, turn left, up steps used earlier and follow the route used earlier, again passing St Mary-le-Bow, the possible site of the White Church where the body of St Cuthbert rested during the building of the cathedral. Turn left along North Bailey, passing the 13th century Chapel of the Nine Altars on the right.

Pass the gateway to the College Green with its early Georgian

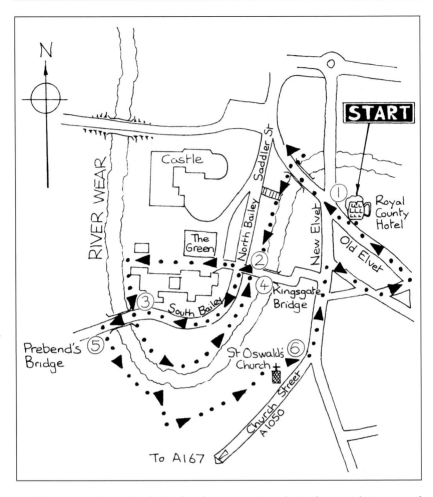

architecture. Here North Bailey becomes South Bailey, with its grand doorways. Go through Watergate Arch, which was erected in 1778. Bear left to cross Prebend's Bridge, rebuilt in 1772 to replace the original which was destroyed by flood in 1771.

⑤ Turn left along a riverside path until just past where a watercourse is bridged. Turn right along a narrow, stepped path which soon contours. At its end, turn left, briefly, then right, over a bridge and along another path, soon to go through a kissing gate. Stay on the path until another watercourse is bridged and immediately turn right up steps. Turn left along another broad path that soon edges a churchyard, where you climb steps on the right and follow the path through the churchyard. Keep left of St Oswald's church, beyond which the path becomes flagged.

St Oswald, King of Northumbria, became a Christian on Iona and invited St Aidan to settle on Lindisfarne to convert his kingdom to Christianity. He died fighting Penda, pagan king of Mercia, in AD 642. His severed head is in St Cuthbert's tomb.

⑥ Leave the churchyard and bear left along a roadside footpath, crossing the road to the right hand one when traffic allows. Continue downhill and, just past Barclay's bank, turn right along Elvet Crescent. Continue along Court Lane, which soon turns sharp left. The road then curves right, then left to join Old Elvet. Turn left along it, soon to pass the old Shire Hall, beyond which, on the right, stands the Royal County Hotel.

Lanchester
The King's Head

Lanchester is surrounded by hilly, well-wooded countryside, which this easy walk explores. For the final mile, the route follows the Lanchester Valley Walk, a disused railway, now a haven for interesting plants and wildlife.

Lanchester is named after the Roman fort of Longovicium, which is on a hillside $1/2$ mile south-west of the village. The fort was built in AD 122 to guard Dere Street, which linked York to Hadrian's Wall.

All Saints' church, with its four-square, battlemented tower, dominates Lanchester. Opposite it, a wide green, adorned with trees, is flanked by prosperous-looking stone houses, shops and the very pleasant King's Head, once the station master's house. Inside this very pleasant Scottish and Newcastle hostelry a comprehensive range of drinks is on offer, including Newcastle Exhibition, Younger's Scotch Bitter, Guinness, John Smith's, Kronenbourg 1664, Miller's and Foster's lager, and Strongbow and Woodpecker cider. The menu, which changes constantly, is as long as your arm with more than 20 main meals from which to choose. Random samples include Mexican chicken fajitas, pork hock and lamb shank with mint gravy. All the steaks from the grill are prime Aberdeen Angus, cooked to perfection and served with onion rings, mushrooms and grilled potato. Sunday lunch is served from 12 noon to 7.30 pm and bar food is available throughout opening times except on Sunday evenings and Sunday lunch times, when the restaurant menu applies.

Telephone: 01207 520054

- **HOW TO GET THERE:** Lanchester is 7 miles north west of Durham City along the A691, where four major roads meet. In the village, where the B6296 branches left just west of All Saints' church, the King's Head is on the left, facing the green.
- **PARKING:** You can park at the rear of the King's Head.
- **LENGTH OF THE WALK:** 4 miles. Maps: OS Explorer 307 and 308 (GR 167474).

THE WALK

① From the King's Head, cross the road and continue across the village green bearing slightly right to the A691, which you go over at a crossing. Turn along a roadside footpath for about 50 yards to turn right at a footpath sign. Go along a short, tarmac lane, using a wayside footpath. At the lane end, cross a wall stile on your left and immediately turn right along a clear path that keeps close to the field's right hand side. Exit through a gap made for a wicket in the right hand corner of a facing hedge. Go straight up the next field, close to its right hand side, following a climbing path that curves left, then right, between shrubs, to reach a stile in the right-hand corner of a facing hedge. Cross the stile and continue straight ahead, close to a ditch and a hedge on the right, then alongside a mix of fence and hedge. From here the retrospective view of Lanchester, in the valley bottom, is very good indeed.

On reaching an almost impenetrable cluster of gorse that fronts a facing fence, turn left alongside it for about 30 yards then bear slightly right and go through a gateway in a step in the fence. Once through it, go diagonally right, up the hillside, following a clear, meandering path that goes through a gap in the gorse bushes to reach a ladder stile in the fence on your right, fronted by more gorse, through which the path goes to meet the stile at a tangent. Cross the ladder stile and go straight

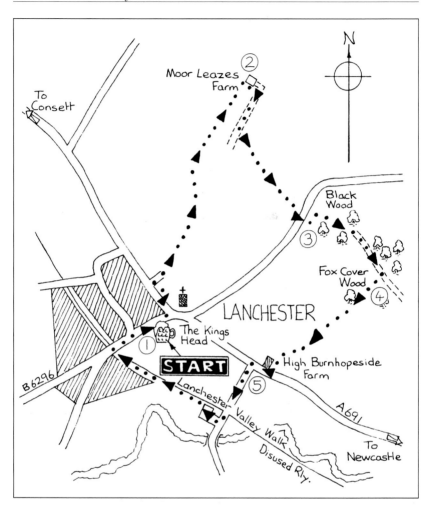

ahead on a clear path that follows a line of telegraph poles towards Moor Leazes Farm.

② Just before some farm buildings, turn right along a track that edges the field.

The countryside hereabouts is most attractive. It is a series of lateral ridges spreading eastwards from the Pennines. The views are very good indeed.

Once the field is edged, go through a facing, waymarked gateway on a farm track and turn right with it, close to a wall on the right. On reaching the end of the field leave the track short of a facing gap and turn left to edge the field close to a hedge on your right. It is a long field and some way along it the hedge ends. Simply continue in the same direction and soon the hedge starts again. Leave the field over a facing right hand corner stile alongside a gate onto the B6296.

③ Immediately turn right for about seven yards keeping close to the road's edge (you are on the inside of a bend). As soon as a footpath sign is seen on the opposite side, cross the road with care. Cross a stile in a step in the hedge and follow a woodland path that descends to cross a stream on a plank bridge. Continue along the path, which now climbs diagonally left between deciduous trees to enter Black Wood, a thin band of tall evergreens. Go straight through it, still on the climbing path, which continues beyond Black Wood, going between a mix of conifers and deciduous trees towards Foxcover Wood ahead.

Short of Foxcover Wood, go diagonally left across a facing farm track to enter the wood along a most pleasant contouring ride, met end on.

Lanchester valley is below you on your right.

④ Soon a group of electricity poles is reached on the right and a descending path is also off to the right. Take it and in a few yards, go right at a fork, descending through woodland, at first alongside the remains of a wall on the left, then keeping just inside the wood, close to a fence on the right. Soon the path turns left, still just inside the wood. In about 25 yards, just short of some conifers, turn right, over a stile into a field. Cross it diagonally right, descending. Exit over a site alongside a gate beneath a large sycamore tree in the field's corner. Turn left edging the next field and, just short of High Burnhopeside Farm, seen ahead, turn left over a stile. Go forward for about 25 yards and, where the fence on the right ends, turn right, down the field to the A691.

⑤ Turn right, along a roadside footpath, and very quickly reach a signpost to Malton, where you turn left, crossing the road with care and continue along a minor one met head on.

Take the first turning right, through the car park of Malton picnic area and continue across the picnic area itself, to join the Lanchester Valley Walk, along a disused railway track, met at a tangent.

Now simply continue along the old trackbed for about a mile to where the B6296 crosses it. Leave the trackbed here, turning right along a street towards the village green, where the King's Head awaits.

Causey Arch
The Causey Arch Inn
❧

The combination of the Tanfield Railway, the world's oldest line built in 1725 to carry coal to the river Tyne, and Causey Arch, the world's oldest surviving railway bridge, now the centrepiece of a spectacular silvan gorge, itself laced with old waggonways, makes this superb walk an unforgettable experience.

From the elevated windows of this traditional, friendly pub there is a splendid view of the surrounding countryside, including the wooded gorge and its splendid masterpiece, Causey Arch.

In the pub's upstairs restaurant, where good food is offered in a friendly, cosy atmosphere, the menu is augmented by the chef's specials, displayed on a blackboard. All the dishes on the menu are home-cooked using the freshest ingredients; and always available are hot and cold sandwiches and specials 'for the little ones'. Lunch is served between 12 noon and 2 pm every day, and evening meals are between 7 pm and 10 pm. Sunday lunch is served from midday onwards when delicious hand-carved roasts and other weekly changing dishes are served. Booking is advised. This is a free house with Theakston Best Bitter and Old Peculier very popular in 'the 19th hole'. Woodpecker and Scrumpy Jack ciders and red and white wines are also on offer. Well-behaved dogs are welcome, and overnight accommodation is available.

Telephone: 01207 233925

- **HOW TO GET THERE:** Take the A6076 southwards from Sunniside towards Stanley. After some 2 miles, you will find the pub occupying an elevated position on the left side of the road.
- **PARKING:** There is a large car park fronting the pub.
- **LENGTH OF THE WALK:** 3½ miles. Map: OS Explorer 308 (GR 207563)

THE WALK

(1) From the Causey Arch Inn cross the A6076 and follow a minor road, met end on. Go over a level crossing and 50 yards beyond turn left into Causey Arch picnic area. Follow a tarmac road across it and just before it exits through a railway arch turn right along a path signposted 'To Causey Arch', passing a toilet on the right.

(2) The path descends a man-made embankment built in 1725 to carry the Tanfield Waggonway, which was powered by horses. Where the path splits, go right, descending, and continue along a path which curves left, passing a footbridge on the right, soon to cross Causey Beck on another footbridge. The path continues upstream, crossing the beck twice more on footbridges, to reach the bottom of Causey Arch, where you turn right, up steps, to the waggonway.

When Ralph Wood, a local stonemason completed Causey Arch in 1727, it was the largest single span bridge in Britain and remained so for 30 years. No one previously had ever built such a bridge and he relied on Roman technology.

A short detour across the bridge is a must, to visit the Tanfield Railway on the other side. Its former wooden rails were replaced by iron ones in 1839. An original wagon stands on the waggonway, which was probably the first major civil engineering of Britain's Industrial Revolution.

Re-cross the bridge and continue along the path, now coinciding with a waggonway. Where it splits, go left, descending, and edging the steep-sided gorge, which becomes shallower the further along it you

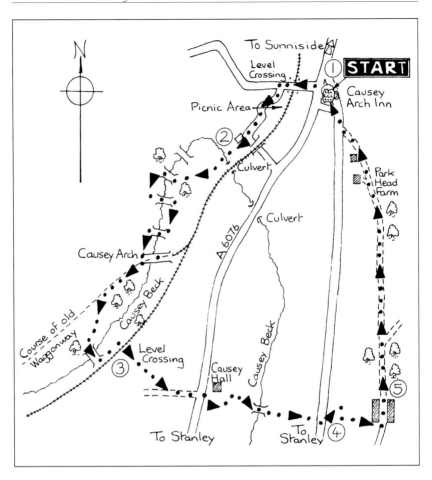

go. On reaching a waymarked footbridge, cross it, turn left, down stream, briefly, then climb a bank. From its top, take the right fork to cross the Tanfield Railway. Go forward, briefly, still on the path, turn left with it, then right and cross a stile into a field.

③ Go along the field's left hand side, uphill, leave through a facing waymarked gateway and descend to a facing track. Turn left along it to the A6076, which you cross. Descend steps at a footpath sign and, at the embankment's foot, turn right as waymarked. In 25 yards, turn left over a stile into a field. Follow a green path edging a hedge on your left with Causey Hall beyond it. Exit over a facing stile in the field's left hand corner. Continue diagonally left, guided by a yellow arrow and on reaching the corner of the Hall's garden, turn right along a clear, descending path, close to the fence on the right. Near the right hand corner, leave the field down steps.

From the bottom step the path goes diagonally right across a narrow field to go over Causey Beck on a waymarked footbridge. The path now bears right then left, to a clearly-seen facing waymarked step-stile. Cross it, climb a steep bank on steps and from the top continue, edging the field's right hand boundary. Exit over a facing stile in its right hand corner onto a minor road.

(4) Turn right along it for 50 yards, then turn left, towards a gateway, but do not go through it. Instead, turn left again, guided by a footpath sign, and go through a gap stile into a wood. Follow a path, diagonally right, through it. Exit over a right-hand stile at the wood's right hand corner, ignoring the facing, waymarked stile. Edge the field ahead alongside a hedge on your left, leaving through a waymarked gap stile at the left hand corner of a facing fence. Go diagonally right across the field ahead leaving through a facing stile in its right-hand corner. Edge the next field close to a right hand fence. Exit over a facing stile and continue along a short lane into Coppy.

Turn left along an unsurfaced road. Where a right hand fork goes through a metal gate, go left through a wicket and along a clear track. Continue ahead on a clear path as it curves left into Park Head Farm, soon to join a concrete track at a tangent. Carry on along it, descending to a minor road. Turn right back to the Causey Arch Inn, seen ahead.

Ebchester

The Derwent Walk Inn

A scenic railway trackbed contouring a lovely river valley in a country park, strong historical associations with the Romans, the romance of the days of steam, a liberal sprinkling of natural history and a welcoming hostelry are irresistible ingredients in this most enjoyable walk.

The Romans built a fort, Vindomora, where Dere Street crossed the river Derwent. Today it is the border village of Ebchester, and you can find there a small museum containing information about the fort. The B6309 climbs steeply south-easterly out of Ebchester and in less than ½ mile it bridges the disused Derwent Valley Railway. Here adjacent to Ebchester station, the Station Hotel stood. It was destroyed in a fire which killed the landlord, was rebuilt in 1947 and later renamed the Derwent Walk Inn.

A refreshing drink or a delicious meal in this award-winning traditional country pub, with unrivalled views across the Derwent

Valley to Northumberland, complements this walk perfectly. There is a beer garden for when the weather is warm and on cold days there is a roaring fire. The pub has a good range of real ales and its Jennings Cumberland ale, Jennings Bitter, Cockermoop and Snedlifter will make your eyes sparkle, just as the menu will make you drool. Roast Lamb Jennings is an all-time favourite from a large menu choc-a-bloc with exquisite choices like oven roasted Barbary duck breast served with peach wedges and a peach and red wine sauce. The salad section includes chicken and goats cheese salad and Cumbrian Cobblers. Then there are the grilled things, with steaks cooked to your liking. By the time you have sampled the food on offer you'll be glad you did the walk first.

Telephone: 01207 560347

- **HOW TO GET THERE:** Take the A691 from Durham city north-westerly, continuing on the B6309 through Leadgate. Where the road descends steeply on approaching Ebchester, short of where the Derwent Valley Railway is bridged, the Derwent Walk Inn is on the right.
- **PARKING:** In the inn's car park.
- **LENGTH OF THE WALK:** 3 miles. Map: OS Explorer 307 (GR 107547).

THE WALK

① From the Derwent Walk Inn, cross the road and turn right along a roadside footpath. Cross a railway bridge and immediately turn left, down some steps and along a short path to the disused Derwent Valley Railway.

The old line ran for 11 miles between Swalwell and Consett and in 1972 the Derwent Walk along its trackbed was opened. Its surface is suitable for cycles, horses and wheelchairs as well as for those on foot.

Turn left along it going under the bridge to pass the site of Ebchester station, now a car park and picnic area. Continue along the trackbed, flat as a pancake hereabouts, as it goes along the top of a very high, wooded embankment, beyond which it descends, then rises, where a bridge has been removed.

The Derwent Valley Walk is the centrepiece of the Derwent Walk Country Park, one of the largest country parks in the north-east of England. The park is always open and contains woodlands, meadows, ponds and riverside.

Stay on the trackbed soon to cross metalled Shaw Lane, continuing along the route of the old railway.

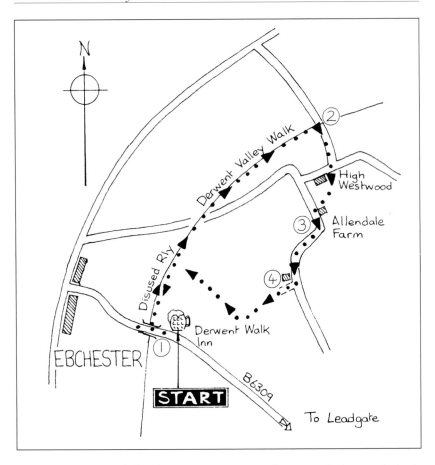

Below, to the left, the river Derwent flows and, beyond it, is Northumberland.

The trackbed continues through woodland where the verges are lush and full of wildlife. Field scabious, rosebay willow herb and foxgloves grow among the silver birches, sycamores, hazels and brambles in a glorious kaleidoscope of colour and form. It is an area frequented by both the green and great spotted woodpecker, nuthatches and the ubiquitous magpies, among many other birds. With luck, roe deer, foxes and even badgers may be glimpsed. These are shy creatures so quietness is of the essence.

On reaching a barrier go through a gap at its side and continue descending a slope to where a lane crosses the trackbed at right angles. When the line was operating there was a bridge here.

The view from the Derwent Walk.

(2) Turn right along the lane, going steeply uphill to the mining hamlet of High Westwood. When a facing minor road is met, cross it diagonally right and bear left at a footpath sign, passing the gable end of a row of dwellings on the right. Continue past the gable end, along a short passage, passing a garden, and cross a stile into a field. Cross the field diagonally right soon to edge the field's right hand side, briefly, before crossing a stile in a facing fence. Go diagonally right across a farm area to a waymarked stile at its right hand corner; cross it onto a road.

(3) Turn left, along it, uphill, passing Allendale Farm on the left. As the road goes straight ahead before turning right, reduce the angle by using a roadside footpath which, for a short distance, follows a more direct but steeper route to the top. There used to be a village, Allandale Cottages, on the top of this hill but little remains.

Continue edging the hill's rim on a roadside footpath until a square brick tower is passed. Just beyond it turn right at a footpath sign and descend to go through a facing gate into a field. Go down a short broad track to the foot of a steep slope and at a fork, go left to a waymarked gate in a fence on your right, met at a tangent.

(4) Keep straight ahead on a broad, clear track for about 100 yards to where a narrow path, faint to begin with, descends at an acute angle,

The Derwent Valley Walk goes through lush woodland.

going slightly right to meet a waymarked stile in a fence on your right. Cross the stile and continue along a field path descending diagonally left. The path becomes more defined further along and cuts through a row of trees. Go diagonally left, undefined, to the field corner. Exit through a kissing gate and go forward briefly to the Derwent Valley Railway trackbed, walked on the outward leg. Turn left along the old line's route and retrace your steps to the Derwent Walk Inn.

Stanhope
The Pack Horse

The well-signposted Weardale Way provides a clear trail to the walk's apex, at which elevated point the true extent of mining and quarrying that took place around Stanhope can be seen and the relationship between industry and agriculture put into perspective. This is a fascinating and airy excursion into yesteryear.

The people of Stanhope do not need to be reminded that their beautiful town is the 'capital of Weardale'. They know this and it makes them swell with justifiable pride and if they had tails they would wag them. For Stanhope, which became wealthy on lead mining, is surrounded by lovely scenery, much of it woodland. Its parish church of St Thomas the Apostle, built around 1200, has a Roman altar in the vestry inscribed *silvano invicto sacrum*, sacred to the unconquered god, Silvanus, the god of the woods. Near the churchyard entrance is a fossilized tree stump which is 256 million years old.

The Pack Horse is not quite as ancient. It is an old coaching establishment without delusions of grandeur. Horses were hitched to an iron bracket fixed to the right of the pub's entrance. During opening hours, from 12 noon to 11 pm, Newcastle brown ale, John Smith's and Tetley brews are served from a well-stocked cellar and taste like good beers should taste.

The food is wholesome and as much as possible of it is home made. Fare such as mince and dumplings, corned beef pie, cod and chips, lasagne, gammon and pineapple is always available, and children's meals are also served.

Telephone: 01388 528407

- **HOW TO GET THERE:** Stanhope is on the A689, some 5^1/$_2$ miles west of Wolsingham. The Pack Horse is on the left hand side of the road in the market place, opposite the parish church.
- **PARKING:** In front of the pub and in the Durham Dales Centre.
- **LENGTH OF THE WALK:** 4^1/$_2$ miles. Maps: OS Explorer 307 and Outdoor Leisure 31 (GR 996393).

THE WALK

① From the Pack Horse turn right, edging the market place, which fronts the church of St Thomas the Apostle.

The present building stands on the site of an earlier wooden one. It has had its share of eminent rectors, no less than eight of whom have become bishops, and has been called 'one of the most perfect and interesting of the ecclesiastical structures of the Middle Ages in the country'.

In a short distance turn right along a descending road that curves right. When almost at its end, turn left along a lane which backs the gardens of cottages on the left and soon edges the river Wear on the right.

② At its end, cross the railway line where it spans the Wear taking care because it is again in use. Continue across the middle of the field ahead, following the Weardale Way. Edge the next field and bear right over a section of a playing field, to regain the river, which you edge for a short distance. On reaching the railway, again where it bridges the river, cross the line and continue close to the water, on your right, along a lane. Exit through a facing kissing gate into a field, which you cross, leaving over a facing, waymarked stile.

③ Turn right along a minor road that soon bridges the river and climbs steeply to go over the railway before turning sharp left. In a

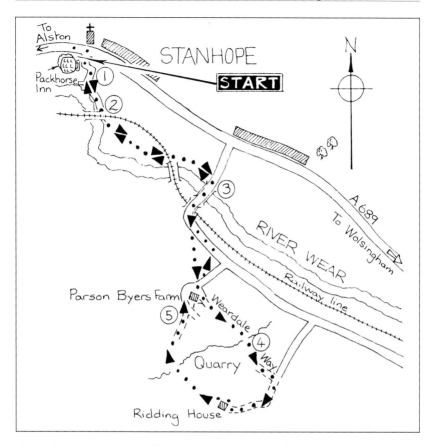

short distance, a row of houses is reached on the left. Here turn right, over a waymarked stile and go diagonally left up the facing field, following a line of telegraph poles along a green track. Leave the field through a stile alongside a facing gate and pass in front of Parson Byers Farm on your right, continuing along a short, gated lane and a farm track.

Below us, on our left, puffs of white smoke caught our attention. It was a train, pulled by a steam engine chuff-chuffing along the Weardale line, evocative of times past.

On reaching a solitary tree, turn right, uphill. As height is gained, a stile comes into view alongside a gateway, in a section of wall on the left. It is waymarked. Cross it and descend, diagonally right, to cross narrow Cow Burn at a Weardale Way marker post. There is no bridge but the beck is narrow.

The fossil tree – it grew about 250 million years ago.

④ Keeping in the same direction, continue over the field and leave over a facing ladder stile. Go diagonally right to the field boundary and turn left alongside it until a stile on the right is reached, which you cross. Immediately turn left along a field track to its end where you turn right, uphill, soon to pass a ruin on the right. At this point the Weardale Way goes left but you stay on the track, which soon curves right, climbing steadily then bears left to reach Ridding House. Go to the right of it, and cross a rough pasture, still on the track. Continue through a facing left-hand corner gate, leaving the track, and gradually edge towards the rim of a huge disused quarry on the right.

Weardale's contribution to the Industrial Revolution was to supply lead ore, iron ore, whinstone and limestone to the fast developing new industries. When cheaper lead became available from abroad around 1890, the mines slid into recession. Today the lead mines and workings and the iron ore and limestone quarries are now reverting to nature and are a fascinating reminder of a very busy past.

Where the fence on your right turns left across your line of walk, turn left with it to descend and cross Cow Burn. Climb the far bank, cross a facing fence and turn right, briefly then left edging the quarry, close to a fence.

Soon, a track is joined. Go along it, at first close to the quarry, but

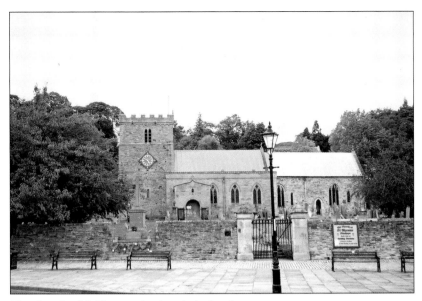

The church of St Thomas the Apostle in Stanhope.

later, where the fence ends, pulling away from it, diagonally left, towards an impressive bank of conifers.

⑤ As the ground falls away, excellent views are revealed. The route then descends to a crossing of tracks: keep straight ahead, descending behind Parson Byers Farm and curving right to regain the outward route. Follow a descending lane with a wall on the right and a fence on the left. At the bottom of the lane, turn left along a minor road, soon to reach the row of dwellings passed on the outward leg. From here retrace your steps to the Pack Horse.

Wolsingham
The Black Bull

❧❀❧

Elephants stamping along the valley's southern rim, trunk holding tail – that is what the famous elephant trees portray. They are seen to advantage from this exhilarating but easy walk through some of Weardale's most fertile land. Nowhere in the dale is lusher than around Wolsingham.

The little town of Wolsingham is pleasantly sited at the eastern approach to Weardale. It has many attractive buildings like Whitfield House, a fine 18th century three storey structure set back from the road behind two holly trees. Whitfield Place, next to it, is long and low, with mullioned windows and is dated 1611.

Built in 1720, the Black Bull was originally an excise office and some of its ceiling beams are original. When built, it was detached and recently, when the gable-end wall of its dining room was exposed, the original stonework was found to contain a deep-set 18th century window. It is a residential hotel, and has two permanent guests – one is a benign ghost and the other his phantom hound. The ghost delights in tapping shoulders and blowing into people's ears.

Fishermen frequently congregate at the Black Bull, where they boast about the size of their catches. When once a fisherman proudly told the landlord he had caught a five pound trout in the River Wear, the landlord said he could beat that for he had recently pulled a twelve stone haddock out of the river. This was quite true. The landlord had, in fact, rescued a twelve stone man from the water and his name was Haddock. The story is recalled in a framed poem at the inn.

Bedroom No 6 is not the only haunted room in the Black Bull. Part of the building was once a coaching house, and many guests claim to have seen a couple walking from room to room.

In the charming olde worlde atmosphere of this welcoming inn appetites are catered for from 12 noon until 2 pm when lunches and snacks are served, and between 7 pm and 9 pm when the restaurant menu offers roast grouse, medallions of beef fillet with a forest mushroom sauce, and tuna steak with red wine sauce among other similar dishes.

Good real ales are available and CAMRA meetings are held here regularly. On a fine day, drinkers can watch the passing scene from the small beer garden that fronts the pub.

Telephone: 01388 527332

- **HOW TO GET THERE:** Wolsingham is on the A689, 14 miles west of Durham City. The Black Bull is on the left, facing the market place as you go westwards up the dale.
- **PARKING:** You can park in the market place, directly across the road from the inn.
- **LENGTH OF THE WALK:** 4 miles. Maps: OS Explorer 307, Outdoor Leisure 31 (GR 077371).

THE WALK

① From the inn turn left along the road and cross to the other side. Just past a road junction on the left, turn right along Church Lane. At the lane end, continue into the churchyard, turning left at the church to a crossing of paths. Turn left, briefly, then right, through a gateway. Go along a lane edging the churchyard, continuing beyond it, past a junction on the right, to reach, but not to go through, a kissing gate. Instead turn left, still on the lane. At its end, go through a kissing gate, then diagonally right, along a field path, edging a fence on the left. Go

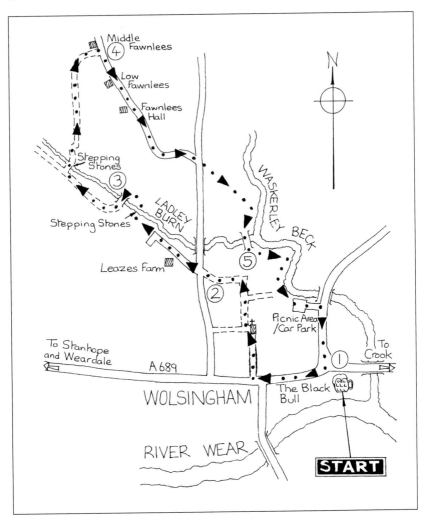

through a kissing gate left of a gate in a step in the fence and continue along a lane beneath a copse of beech, chestnut and the odd Scots pine.

② Soon a minor road is crossed. Continue along a lane, signposted to Leazes Farm.

The elephant trees really do look like elephants from here.

The lane goes to the right of the farm. Just before it turns sharp left, go right, through a waymarked kissing gate, and immediately turn left. Continue along a bank top above Ladley Burn on the right, following a clear green path. It soon curves and descends, becoming very broad. Cross a waymarked stile left of a facing gate and cross Ladley Burn on stepping stones. Immediately go left, upstream, along a green path, directed by an arrow. Climb a stile to the right of a facing gate in to woodland.

③ Recross the stream on a footbridge and follow a lane which curves right, edging woodland on the right.

In springtime the stream on the right gurgles merrily between shading trees that rise from an indigo coverlet of bluebells, spangled with cowslips and pale primroses. Come autumn, these same trees are fired with glorious autumn colours as their leaves await their fall. To the left of the lane sheep in lush pastures nibble contentedly at juicy grasses blissfully unaware of mint sauce.

On reaching a junction, turn right, as waymarked, down a short lane. Go through a facing gate and again cross the stream on stepping stones. Go diagonally right, up a facing bank, and edge the field on a climbing track, close to a fence on the right. Leave it through a facing gate and edge the next one, close to a wall on your right. Exit through a gate, set back on your right, into a walled lane.

From here, the long view down the valley is a glorious blend of greens and browns of every hue.

Pass Middle Fawnlees farm on the left and go through a gate into a walled lane.

④ Turn right along the lane, passing first Low Fawnlees and then Fawnlees Hall, beyond which the lane turns left, soon to reach a minor road, which you cross. Go through a signposted kissing gate and edge the next two fields on a clear path, with a hedge on your right, to reach Wasterley Beck. Turn right, along a beckside path.

⑤ Soon cross Ladley Burn near to its confluence with Wasterley Beck, on a footbridge. Cross the field ahead, as waymarked, as far as a facing stile on your left. Continue down stream on a clear green path. Exit through a facing kissing gate into a long narrow picnic area that edges Wasterley Beck. Bear right through the picnic area to a car park, continuing between it and Wasterley Beck, following a clear path which soon meets the approach to the car park at a tangent.

Continue along this short car park approach road, turn right at a road junction, through Wolsingham, past the market place and back to the Black Bull.

Langdon Beck
The Langdon Beck Hotel
۶❧৶

On this splendid airy circular in Teesdale's lonely upper reaches you have for company the magnificent heights of Cronkley Scar and Widdy Bank Fell, with its abundance of birdlife. The landscape is wild and exhilarating but the route is undemanding and easily walked.

Langdon Beck would have suited Greta Garbo for there are few lonelier places in County Durham. The road across Langdon Fell to St John's Chapel, in Weardale is, at 1,056 ft. above sea level, the highest classified road in England. The hamlet, consisting of some isolated farms and smallholdings, a small church, a school, a youth hostel and a pub, is loosely scattered around Langdon Common, one of the wildest places in the country.

Across the road from the Langdon Beck Hotel is a building which used to be a coaching house. In 1887, when the present pub was built, the coaching house licence was transferred to it. With Cross Fell, the highest point in the Pennines, only a few miles away, the Langdon Beck Hotel needs to be able to withstand the ravages of a harsh winter – and it is. Stone-built and strong enough to shake off the worst of storms, its bar is snug and a real refuge. The dining room is larger, well able to seat a bus load of people at a time. It is a freehouse that specialises in providing good, wholesome food at reasonable prices. Food is served from 11.30 am to 2.30 pm Monday to Saturday and 12 noon to 1.30 pm on Sunday. It is also available between 7 pm and 9 pm each evening. Opening hours at the bar are from 11 am to 3 pm and 7 pm to 11 pm Monday to Saturday and from 12 noon to 2 pm and 7 pm to 10.30 pm on Sunday. The pub has a beer garden and a garden area for children.

Telephone: 01833 622267

- **HOW TO GET THERE:** The Langdon Beck Hotel is on the left-hand side of the B6277 when approached from Middleton-in-Teesdale, where the road makes a sharp right turn followed by a left-hand one, having crossed the bridge over Langdon Beck.
- **PARKING:** You can park on the pub forecourt or in an adjacent car park.
- **LENGTH OF THE WALK:** $3^1/_2$ miles. Map: Outdoor Leisure 31 (GR 854313).

THE WALK

(1) From the Langdon Beck Hotel turn right along a minor road which edges Langdon Beck and, on reaching a confluence with Harwood Beck, turns right alongside the latter. In a short distance, immediately after the road bridges Harwood Beck, turn left along a riverside path, downstream, to Intake Farm.

Many Upper Teesdale lead miners were allowed by the local landowners to claim enclosures on the edge of moorland as smallholdings. There were lots of them and they became known as 'intakes'. Farms with that name are quite common.

A ford crosses Harwood Beck slightly upstream of its meeting with Langdon Beck. Should the water level be low enough, and it usually is, you can eliminate the road walking to the bridge, described above, simply by crossing the ford.

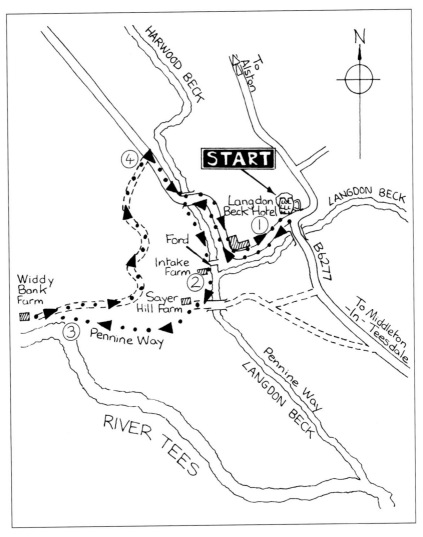

② The path goes between the farm and the beck into a small paddock then turns left briefly to exit through a wicket on the left, back to the beckside. Turn right, at first on low-lying ground, then, as a steep bank rises ahead, go diagonally left, up it. Continue downstream, at first high above it, then descend gradually and continue along the bank and go through a gate in a facing wall. Go diagonally left to join the Pennine Way near Saur Hill Bridge.

The Pennine Way at its roughest toughest, follows an exhilarating route through Upper Teesdale. This section of the walk cuts through some real walking country between High Force and, upstream, Cauldron Snout. Heather-clad moorland, dominated by Cross Fell, is close by, to the west.

Turn right, along the farm road, to nearby Sayer Hill Farm and, on reaching it, bear left, as waymarked, on rising ground, which soon levels out. Then descend slightly to a step stile in a facing wall to the right of a lonely tree, and go diagonally right across rough pasture dropping at first, then climbing to leave the rough pasture over a stile in a facing wall, close to a nature reserve notice.

The nature reserve covers 74 square kilometres and is the largest in England. It rises to 2,782 feet.

The bedrock over most of Widdybank Fell, prominent ahead, and Crokley Fell, across the Tees, is either of the Lower Carboniferous Age, some limestone, some sandstone or shale, or is quartz-dolerite of the Great Whin Sill. As well as providing Upper Teesdale with superb scenery, the Great Whin Sill has formed the cliffs and rocky slopes, screes and riverside banks that are so important as habitats for many species which are unable to compete in closed vegetation.

Follow a green path, diagonally right, guided by a marker post, aiming for the as yet unseen River Tees.

③ On reaching the river bank, bear right to cross a facing stile and continue upstream to a second stile, beyond which go diagonally right alongside a wall on your right. On reaching a gate in the wall, go through it and immediately turn left to Widdy Bank Farm.

Here the Pennine Way is left to continue along perhaps its most exciting section along the boulder-strewn foot of Falcon Clints to Cauldron Snout, two miles distant. This most spectacular cataract falls in a series of eight steps. It is haunted, we are told, by the song of a local girl who, rejected by a lead miner returning to his wife, threw herself into the foaming torrent. The sound is like that of a singing skylark.

The layout of Widdy Bank Farm is typical of many Upper Teesdale farmsteads. It is a Norse shippen with barn, byre and farmhouse all under one roof. Refreshments can be obtained here, but, should they not be required do not enter the farmyard. Instead, turn right, along the farm road, which skirts Widdybank Pasture, at first in a north westerly direction then taking a generally northerly route.

More that 83 species of birds have been recorded as nesting in and around the Upper Teesdale Nature Reserve, of which Widdybank Fell

Langdon Beck.

is a large part. Perhaps the easiest to recognise is the red grouse. During the nesting season there is probably no area in Britain that harbours such a variety of waders as this wild and wonderful upland. The most common bird is the lapwing, but the curlew, with it liquid call, the drumming snipe, the common sandpiper, which has a trilling chatter, the golden plover, oyster catcher and redshank are all at home on these marshy rough pastures and in the wet places of the higher fells. All three wagtails nest commonly in Upper Teesdale, but the most abundant bird is the meadow pipit.

④ In just over a mile, at the farm road's end, turn right along a minor road, with Harwood Beck on the left. Soon the beck is crossed on the bridge used on the outward leg (if you didn't cross at the ford). From there retrace your steps to the Langdon Beck Hotel.

Forest-In-Teesdale
The High Force Hotel

The whole of this area is a mecca for walkers, whether they are in search of a quiet ramble along the Tees or a more demanding trek. The riverside section of this route, which includes the falls at both High Force and Low Force, coincides with the Pennine Way, but all of it is easily walked.

The impressive stone-built High Force Hotel is situated in the unspoilt valley of Upper Teesdale directly opposite an easily negotiated path to High Force, the country's highest above-ground waterfall (the highest in the country is underground at Gaping Gill). It was constructed in the early 19th century by the dukes of Cleveland as a shooting lodge and looks for all the world like two buildings with identical gable ends facing the road, joined by a long section in the middle. It is now a friendly, family-run hotel, warmed by blazing fires in the winter months.

Among the main course dishes on both lunchtime and evening

menus are roast chicken, crisp battered cod, sirloin and gammon steaks and Yorkshire pudding filled with Teesdale sausages and gravy. There is also a 'specials' board. Toasties, sandwiches and jacket potatoes are available and children have their own menu. Food is available all week from 12 noon to 2.30 pm and in the evening from 7 pm to 9.30 pm on weekdays and until 9 pm on Sunday. During the winter months drinks are served from 11 am to 4 pm and 7 pm to 11 pm Monday to Saturday with usual Sunday hours. During the summer months coffee is served from 10 am and the bar is open from 11 am until 11 pm. Among the draught ales is the award winning Cauldron Snout ale, which won the North East beer of the year award for 2000. There is a full range of guest beers and draught cider and wines are also available. The hotel has a children's certificate for the whole of the premises and there are picnic tables and an ice cream kiosk outside.

Telephone: 01833 622222

- **HOW TO GET THERE:** The High Force Hotel stands in solitary splendour beside the B6277, 5 miles north west of Middleton-In-Teesdale.
- **PARKING:** In front of the hotel or in an adjoining public car park.
- **LENGTH OF THE WALK:** $3^1/_2$ miles, including a detour to High Force. Map: Outdoor Leisure 31 (GR 885286).

THE WALK

(1) From the High Force Hotel go diagonally left across the B6277 and bear left along the roadside footpath, briefly to a footpath sign, where you turn right along a stepped path, descending a wooded bank that edges the Tees. The steps have metal banisters to ease progress. Exit the wood through a wicket and continue downstream, edging a field along a green path. Go through a kissing gate, turn right and cross the Tees on Holwick Bridge.

Immediately turn left for a few yards, cross a facing stile and, continue downstream, crossing stiles until Low Force is passed and, just below it, the Wynch Bridge is reached.

Here, where a dry stone wall approaches the river at right angles, a sculpture depicting two sheep stands on the wall top.

Botanists drool over this part of the river where the delicate, pink bird's eye primrose, bog sandwort, yellow globe flower, rockrose, deep blue spring gentian and shrubby cinquefoil grow. At least 150 species of rare plants bloom hereabouts.

Low Force, also known as Little Force or Salmon Leap, is much

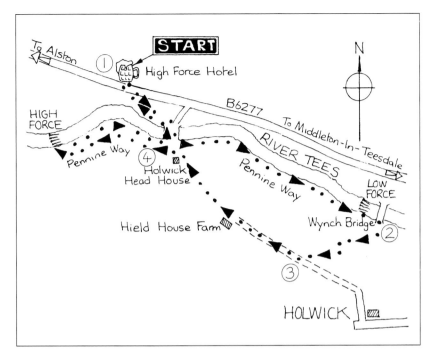

favoured by visitors. Below this series of low falls the river surges through a narrow gorge and the current is dangerous.

The Wynch Bridge spans the gorge. Opened in 1830, it replaces an older one dated 1704, which was used by miners. Thought to be the first suspension bridge in Europe, it had a handrail on one side only and few strangers dared trust themselves to cross it. In 1803 the main chain broke while some miners were crossing and one man was drowned.

② From the Wynch Bridge take a path downstream briefly, to a kissing gate and continue along a clear path that curves right, away from the river. At the end of a wooded bank on your right turn right, directed by a yellow arrow. In a short distance cross a section of broken wall, continue over the next field, passing a waymarker on a post, and keep straight ahead to cross a waymarked ladder stile. Edge the field ahead, close to a wall on the right. Just past where the stream on your left turns left, do likewise to cross a small concrete bridge.

A proliferation of golden marsh marigolds, or king cups, adorns this area from March to July.

Go forward to join a farm track, at first alongside a wall on the left, to a ruin, where the track curves right to leave the field though a facing gate. Continue along the track to meet a farm road at right angles.

③ Turn right, along it, soon passing to the right of Hield House Farm and going through a facing gate. Continue close to the wall on the right, go through a gate at the right hand corner of a facing wall and cross the next field still close to the wall. Leave through another facing gateway. Cross the next field on a farm track, towards Holwick Head House, seen ahead.

Here heartsease, blue , yellow and two-tone, carpet the route, at their best during June and July.

Cross a step stile alongside a facing gate and where the path splits at the farmhouse, go right, descending to the foot of the bank.

④ A detour to the left from here, up a stepped path, to see High Force is a must. From the farm just passed, the path's left fork that fronts it, is not a right of way. You must go down the bank, turn left at its foot and climb back up it.

The detour follows a well-maintained path between junipers soon to edge the gorge into which the river plunges over High Force. Extreme caution is needed on this section. The roar of High Force is heard long before you see this spectacular phenomenon. The river crosses a thick layer of igneous dolerite rock, known locally as whinstone, and plunges 80 feet into a pool at the head of a wooded gorge. It is one of the most dramatic drops in the country. It is part of the Upper Teesdale National Nature Reserve and 150,000 people visit it annually.

Retrace your steps first to Holwick Bridge, which you cross, then back upstream to the High Force Hotel.

Hamsterley
The Cross Keys

With open countryside spread around like a patchwork quilt, the River Wear following a north to south-east course nearby and the great forest of Hamsterley stretching into the western distance (and with narry a hint of urban Witton Park and Toft Hill just a few miles away) it is not surprising that this most pleasing of field and lane walks is so popular.

The pleasant village of Hamsterley sits on top of a hill surrounded by a patchwork of open countryside, its delightful dwellings arranged along both sides of a long street above a slanting green at its middle. At its rural heart, the village pub, the Cross Keys, offers patrons a warm welcome. It is a snug haven where dominoes and darts can be enjoyed in a lounge with gleaming brasses and polished woodwork. Fine home-made food is a speciality of this delightful hostelry, and the comprehensive menu includes peppered sirloin, poultry dishes like South Sea Island chicken, vegetable provençale and fresh, crispy salads. Meals are served every lunchtime and evening with special

Sunday lunches. John Smith's and Stone's bitter, Beamish stout, real ales, Scrumpy Jack cider, and red and white wines are all on draught. The inn has a beer garden and a play area for children. Contented doves living in the substantial dovecote in the beer garden sum up the happy atmosphere with a succession of effusive 'coos'.

Telephone: 01388 488457

- **HOW TO GET THERE:** Take the A68 northwards from West Auckland, turn left at High Etherley, still on the A68, and after 2½ miles, just short of crossing the River Wear, turn left as signposted to Hamsterley and within 2 miles there you are. The Cross Keys is on the right, just beyond the village green.
- **PARKING:** There is a large car park for patrons at the rear of the pub.
- **LENGTH OF THE WALK:** 3½ miles. Map: Outdoor Leisure 31 (GR 117311).

THE WALK

(1) From the Cross Keys turn left, briefly, then left again, between dwellings, directed by a footpath sign. In a few yards go over a stile to the left of a facing gate into a field, which you cross along a green path. Exit through a broad gap in a facing hedge and go down the middle of a long, narrow field. Exit through a facing, waymarked gap stile and descend steps into a lane. Turn right along it and in a few yards, short of a facing gate into Adder Wood, turn left along a short, clear path which leads to a facing, waymarked wicket, which you go through.

From here, to westwards, can be seen Bedburn where David Bellamy, the famous naturalist, used to live.

Keep straight ahead, down the facing field, and on approaching the bottom of the field, bear right to a clearly seen facing waymarked wicket. Go through it and continue descending along a wide lane dotted with trees, following a clear path. The lane is fenced on the left and walled on the right. Behind the wall lies Adder Wood, once home to adders, hence its name. There are no adders around here today, so you are quite safe.

In the autumn before the deciduous leaves fall they change colour, adding a mellow glow to the countryside that is a joy to see.

Soon a gap in a facing fence identified by a blue arrow is reached. Go through the gap and continue along the wooded lane, still following the path. As progress is made the valley bottom is reached and the path levels and passes Snape Gate farm on the left.

(2) The path now leaves the lane through a gate on the right into a field, which goes alongside Bedburn Beck on a narrow, green path. On

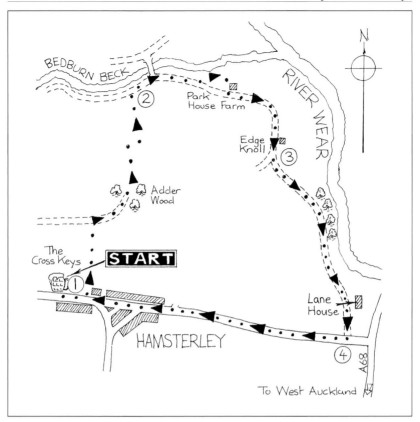

reaching a facing gate in the fence on the left, go through it and follow a woodland track which quickly joins another track at a tangent. Continue along it, parallel to but out of sight of Bedburn Beck, soon the track leaves the woodland continuing downstream soon to pass a private bridge, where a clear farm road is joined. Continue along it, still edging Bedburn Beck, which hereabouts is quite broad. When in spate it is fast flowing, angry and flecked with off-white spume.

On reaching a facing gate go through it and immediately leave the farm road turning left, along a clear path, at first alongside the beck, then curving right and climbing through woodland. Edge a facing lawn, a right of way, and go through a waymarked gate to reach Park House Farm. Bear left, between dwellings, and continue along a farm road through some very scenic country, lush and well-endowed with hedges and trees. The farm road curves left, then sharp right, soon passing Edge Knoll Farm on the left. Here the farm road turns right.

You might spot yellow hammers here – they will warm your heart.

③ Just past Edge Knoll Farm, the farm road skirts the well-named Rabbit Hill on the right, then turns left and continues, straight as an arrow, towards a facing band of woodland by the River Wear. On reaching this woodland, it bears right, climbing, then levels, soon to turn left briefly, then right. In a short distance, Lane House is passed on the left and, a little further on, a cross roads is reached.

A skein of geese flew overhead in 'V' formation when I was last here, each bird getting extra lift from the slip-stream of the bird in front. Like other birds geese choose the easiest conditions for flight. The stronger the prevailing wind, the lower they fly. When a gale is blowing they stick to walking or staying where they are.

④ Turn right at the cross roads along the road to Hamsterley, which climbs steadily. There is a good mile still to go and it is all uphill, but the views are good and underfoot the tarmac is firm.

As Hamsterley looms ahead St James' church is glimpsed through the trees on the left. Then the village embraces you, and, as you walk through it, the Cross Keys comes into view. It is a good moment. You have a good walk behind you and a well deserved meal ahead. As the inn's doves would say 'Coo', or perhaps 'Cor!'.

Romaldkirk

The Rose and Crown

The Tees enters one of its most attractive spots below Egglestone, near Romaldkirk. This walk edges the river at this particular part of its course, well away from any roads so the only way to see it is on foot – and it will be very rewarding.

There are few villages in England prettier than Romaldkirk. Its lovely houses and quaint cottages are set around two well-kept greens where the stocks and water pump still stand, and the church of St Romald, the 'Cathedral of the Dale,' has watched over it since Saxon days.

The Rose and Crown, which is residential, was built in 1733 – the days of coaches and four – and much of it remains unchanged. The charm of those days of old endures in the panelled restaurant, the crackling fire in winter, and its copper and brass and, having sampled Romaldkirk's glorious countryside, how good it is to enjoy an exceptionally good meal in the Rose and Crown's celebrated restaurant, then relax in one of the most hospitable bars imaginable.

Telephone: 01833 650213

- **HOW TO GET THERE:** Romaldkirk is 6 miles north-west of Barnard Castle on the B6277. Where the road edges the village, turn right, briefly, and the pub is on the left.
- **PARKING:** Adequate parking is available for patrons in the pub car park.
- **LENGTH OF THE WALK:** 2^1/$_2$ miles. Map: Outdoor Leisure 31 (GR 995222).

THE WALK

① From the Rose and Crown go diagonally left, across first the road, then the village green, then turn left along another tarmac road that fronts a row of cottages on the right. Soon the Kirk Inn is passed on the left. Just past it, turn right, directed by a Teesdale Way sign, along a lane, between buildings.

The lane, pleasantly lined with tall trees, leads, straight and true, south-easterly. At the lane end go through the left hand of two facing gates into a field with a copse in that corner. Go through the copse and continue for a short distance alongside the wall on the right, as far as a gate. Here go diagonally left along a green path, soon to reach a wicket in a facing hedge, which you go through. Continue, diagonally right now, across the next field, still on a clear, green path, to exit through a gap stile in a facing hedge. Descend a steep slope to join a track and go left, along it, as it curves right to pass in front of Low Garth farm on the left, beyond which you cross a facing step stile.

② Immediately turn left alongside the wall on your left and continue past it, bearing slightly right along a clear path towards the Tees. On approaching the wooded riverside, the path swings right and leads to a facing stile to the right of a gate, which you cross into woodland. Continue, bearing right, along a clearly defined wooded path, parallel to but at first out of sight of the river then edging alongside it.

Rushing along its rocky bed in a turmoil of white spray, then gliding smoothly across a dark dub to break into more rough water as it makes a spectacular change of course, the Tees hereabouts is magnificent. Forget-me-nots, summertime campions and fungi adorn its banks.

The path rounds the bend of the river, descends to cross rocks and

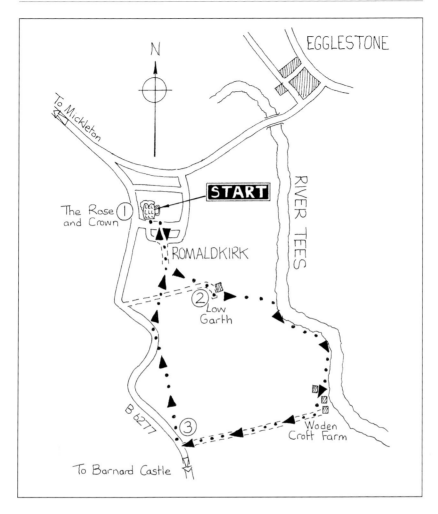

continues edging the river, a delight to walk and easy to follow. In a short distance it widens slightly and cuts a swathe along a tree covered bank. From here, now gravelled and twice its original width, the path climbs a bank, passing a Teesdale Way symbol on a post.

Near the bank's top, cross a stile and continue along the path for a few yards and go through a facing gate. Cross the field ahead on a track alongside a fence on the left, towards Woden Croft Farm, seen ahead. Leave the field at a facing stile, pass some farm buildings on the right and continue along a gravel track alongside the farmhouse on the left.

Woden Croft Lodge, the last building beyond the farmhouse, was once a boarding school of the sort portrayed by Charles Dickens in *Nicholas Nickleby*. One famous old boy was Richard Cobden, who spent five years of his school life here. In 1839 he became a founder of the Anti-Corn Law League, pioneering modern methods of political agitation. The League forced Sir Robert Peel to reduce duty on imported grain to a nominal one shilling a quarter to provide cheap food for urban factory workers. The result was that English farmers could not compete and many had to sell up.

Short of Woden House Lodge turn right through a gate and follow a farm track across the field ahead. The track soon bears left to edge woodland.

③ On reaching a facing gate go through it and turn right, briefly, along the B6277. In about 20 yards, turn right at the footpath sign and go through a kissing gate into a field.

Go diagonally left across the field, aiming for a step stile on the right hand side of a gate in a facing hawthorn hedge.

There are strip lynchets hereabouts, and the terraces formed from this ancient method of cultivation are some 800 feet long and from 15 feet to 40 feet wide.

Continue diagonally left across the field ahead and cross the step in the facing fence. Keep in the same direction, aiming for a clearly seen gap stile in a wall on your left. Go through it to rejoin the B6277. Turn right along it and, where it curves left, cross a triangular grassy area and go over a step stile in a facing wall. Continue alongside the fence on your right and exit the field, over a waymarked step stile in the field's right hand corner. Skirt round the next field and go through the gate in the wall on your right. Retrace your steps to the Rose and Crown.

WALK 11

Bowes

The Ancient Unicorn

Nibbling sheep and browsing cattle in walled fields are a common sight along this easy and exciting walk. Overhead, a flock of curlews emphasised the charm of birds and some banded Galloways and a hunting fox highlighted the variety of the countryside.

Bowes is a quiet village on the western edge of expansive Bowes Moor and stands where the Romans sited a fort, 'Lavatrae', to protect their route westwards over wild Stainmore. Charles Dickens used Bowes School as a model for Dotheboys Hall in *Nicholas Nickleby*. The school's headmaster, William Shaw, becomes Wackford Squeers in that famous novel. Dickens stayed at the Ancient Unicorn while researching for the book and he depicts it as the place where the coach carrying the schoolboys stopped.

Built in the 16th century, this substantial pub, fronted by a cobbled square, has always been a coaching inn and today's visitors are attracted by the relaxed atmosphere and the salubrious fare, much with a South African flavour. For a new brilliant South African chef has introduced a blend of the exotic with all the virtues of local produce. The mouth-watering menu includes gastronomic treats like Bobotle, with rice, carpet-bagger steak stuffed with smoked oysters, Boerewoks (South African sausage) with mash and seafood gratin; and there's lots, lots more. Younger Best Scotch, McEwan's Export, Theakston Bitter and Strongbow cider are the drinks on tap and there is a fine selection of wine. Food is served from Tuesday to Saturday evenings from 6 pm to 9 pm and lunch from 12 noon to 2 pm. The pub is closed on Monday afternoon. The Ancient Unicorn is residential and has a beer garden and play area for children; but no dogs please.

Telephone: 01833 628321

● **HOW TO GET THERE:** From Barnard Castle take the A67 westwards for 4^1/$_2$ miles to meet the A66 as it bypasses Bowes. Go under the bypass and turn left, briefly, then turn right at the crossroads. As you climb through the village, the Ancient Unicorn is on the right.

- **PARKING:** You can leave your car in the pub's square forecourt.
- **LENGTH OF THE WALK:** 5 miles. Map: Outdoor Leisure 30 (GR. 996135).

THE WALK

(1) From the Ancient Unicorn turn right through the village passing St Giles' church on the left. On reaching a 'Bowes Castle' sign, turn left, along a lane, with the castle on the right.

The castle was built by the Normans around 1175 to protect the English against the invading Scots, and then Robert the Bruce destroyed it around 1322. Today only the keep and a grassy moat remain.

Soon the lane curves left, going between the churchyard and a cemetery. Just past the cemetery turn right, over a stile, directed by a footpath sign. Descend the field ahead diagonally left, exiting over a stile three-quarters of the way down the wall on the left. Continue diagonally right across the next field, exiting at a waymarked stile three-quarters of the way along a facing fence. Descend a bank on a narrow path, which curves left to join a track. Turn left along it, edging the River Greta to an unclassified road. Turn right over the bridge and, in a short distance, turn left through a kissing gate at a footpath sign.

(2) Go straight ahead, crossing four fields, using clearly seen stiles, the third one waymarked. Continue over a fifth field, at first close to a wall on the left, then bearing slightly right to cross a clearly seen, waymarked stile in a facing fence.

Follow a clear path between trees, cross a ghyll on a footbridge, climb a bank and exit over a facing stile. Go diagonally right over the next field, leaving at the left hand corner of a fence on your right. Immediately turn left along a track, directed by a yellow arrow.

In a short distance the track crosses How Low Gill on an embankment over a culvert. Once over this feeder, turn right, directed by a yellow arrow and go diagonally left up the field to its left hand corner and to the left of Howlugill Farm. Cross the insulated part of an electrified fence and turn left briefly, along a farm track. In a few yards, where the track turns right, keep ahead, bearing right to leave the field through a facing stile. Cross the field ahead, exit over a facing stile and cross the next field parallel to a line of trees on your right. Where the trees end, continue ahead, directed by a yellow arrow on a telegraph pole. Cross a narrow wood, go over a stile in a facing wall, beyond which there is a farm building. Go diagonally

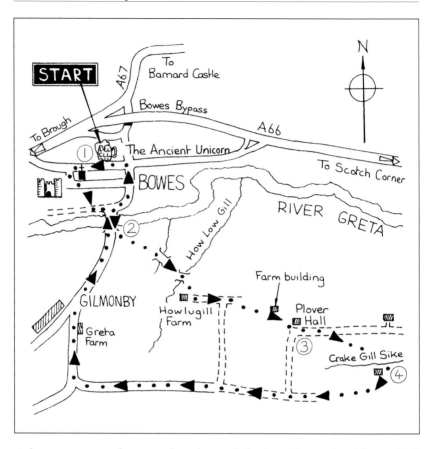

right to a tarmac farm road and turn left along it passing Plover Hall Farm on the left.

③ Continue along this gated road and, short of White Close Hill Farm seen ahead, go diagonally right, directed by a yellow arrow and a signpost. Cross a rough pasture aiming for a solitary tree seen ahead to the left of a group of trees, on reaching it, cross a ladder stile on its left, in a wall met at a tangent.

Go straight ahead alongside a fence on your right, cross Crake Gill Sike on stepping stones, climb a bank, pass to the left of West Ling Farm buildings and cross a stile in a facing wall onto moorland.

Here a herd of banded Galloways cast doleful eyes on us.

④ Go forward for a few yards and turn right along a green path, edging the moor. Keep left of a wood then continue diagonally left, following the path, now a green sward between heather. There are

Belted Galloways near Howlugill Farm.

some marshy bits here and there, which add to the fun and are easily circumnavigated.

On reaching a gate in a facing wall, go through it and continue along a broad, green lane, which offers excellent views across the surrounding countryside. Where a fence crosses the green lane, go through a gateway in it. Continue along the lane, which now has a tarmac surface. On reaching a junction with an unclassified road, turn right, along it.

Pass Greta Farm on the right and some dwellings at Gilmonby on the left. Soon you will meet the signposted kissing gate used on the outward leg. Stay on the road, retracing your steps across the bridge over the River Greta. Continue to a crossroads where you turn left into Bowes where the Ancient Unicorn is on the right.

Barnard Castle
The Golden Lion

৵৻৵

This outstanding arboreal walk is a glorious blend of national and natural history. The town's castle, which has attracted writers and artists, including Scott, Turner and Cotman, dominates the skyline at the walk's start. One of the largest castles in the north, it has enjoyed a chequered but largely peaceful existence. Guy de Baliol built it around 1100 and his family instituted the Oxford college. The riverside path is pure delight, always close to the River Tees which flows, sometimes smoothly, sometimes in a turmoil of white spray, along a meandering course. The woodland, in season, is alive with melodious birdsong, flowers peep shyly from unexpected places and there is a heady sense of freedom.

Barnard Castle is a venerable town of great charm. It is set about a cliff top castle and two wide streets, Calgate and Market Street, lead from near the castle entrance at right angles to each other. Both are lined with 18th century stone houses and an 18th century market cross dominates the southern end of Market Place. Perhaps the most astonishing of all Barnard Castle's buildings is Bowes Museum a magnificent 19th century French château. Set in a 21 acre park, with gardens, tennis courts and a bowling green, it stares imperiously towards the moors of County Durham. A constant surprise, no matter how often you see it, the museum houses some 10,000 beautiful objets d'art in its 22 exhibition rooms, including paintings by El Greco, Goya, Boucher and Canaletto.

The Golden Lion, thought to be the second oldest hotel in 'Barney', was built in 1679. One of its walls was originally part of the castle's curtain wall. The castle's stables are now the Golden Lion's cellars. This very pleasant and well-run hostelry is residential. Its varied menu includes mushroom stroganoff, Cajun chicken, chilli con carne and a very popular breakfast stopper. Snacks and 'lite-bites' are available, as are baguettes, jacket potatoes, toasted sandwiches, and a children's menu. Fungi and veggi-burgers are but two of the burger bar's offerings. Beverages like hot chocolate, tea, coffee, café latte and cappuccino are always available. Marsden's beers, Cameron's creamy smooth and Carlsberg lagers, amongst other drinks, await you at the bar. A magnificent, ancient fireplace takes pride of place in the lounge. It is lit from October throughout the winter months and gives out a cheerful warmth while you savour your chosen tipple.

Telephone: 01833 690333

● **HOW TO GET THERE:** Barnard Castle lies on the A67 some 15 miles west of Darlington. The Golden Lion is in Market Street, on its western side, near the market place.

● **PARKING:** Space in front of the hotel is limited, but there is a public parking area on the opposite side of Market Street.

● **LENGTH OF THE WALK:** 3 miles. Map: Outdoor Leisure 31 (E) (GR 050166).

THE WALK

(1) From the Golden Lion turn right along Market Place, passing the market cross on your left. As you go downhill, a 16th century house is passed on the left. Cromwell was entertained there in 1648, and local magistrates celebrated the accession of James II there. Turn right at a road junction, along the A67.

(2) Where the road turns left over Barnard Castle Bridge, continue straight ahead along a climbing path.

The bridge dates from 1569 – the plaque says 1596 but this is incorrect – and until 1771 illicit marriages took place in the bridge's chapel.

Where the path divides, go left, descending, then edging the river, through woodland. Soon a pipe bridge is passed. Continue upstream

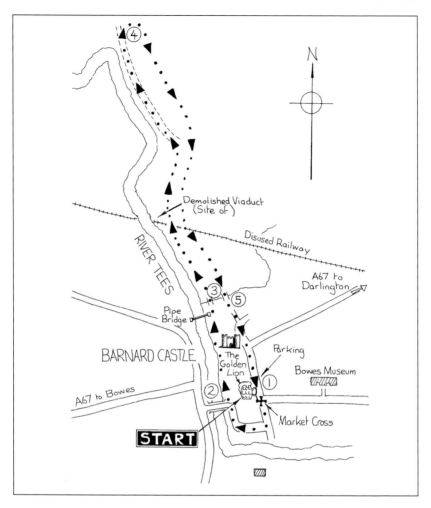

on the clear path that curves right, briefly, then left, over a feeder, then returns to the river bank.

③ Slightly upstream of the feeder are six seats, favoured by ancients and young lovers alike. The path rises, then contours, going between trees where, in springtime, primroses, anemones, bluebells and violets bloom. Ignore a narrow path which branches right and continue on the main path. At a fork, after some distance, take the right, broader, ascending path, stepping over exposed roots and stones that add a sense of adventure to every step.

Having climbed some 300 feet above the Tees, the path reaches the stone buttress of a viaduct, now demolished, that once carried the railway line from Barnard Castle over Stainmore to Kirkby Stephen. It was one of the most scenic lines in the country. The views from here are magnificent.

Do not go in front of the buttress. Instead, continue through the buttress arch and follow a clear path along the wooded bank. Soon it does a sharp right turn, briefly, before turning left and continues contouring until a clear T-junction with another path is reached. Turn right along this path and stay on it, ignoring any side tracks as it climbs to a facing fence at the bank's top.

This is the apex of this lovely walk.

④ Turn right alongside the fence on a clear path, slippery in parts after rain, soon to cross the trackbed of the disused railway near the viaduct buttress. Yellow arrows set at intervals confirm your route. Ignoring other paths stay with the one alongside the wire on your left. For some distance path and fence remain side by side, then the path eases away from the fence and descends gently.

In a short distance, a path branches away on the right, descending steeply. Ignore it and keep straight ahead as the path you are on becomes wider. Soon the path curves left into a side valley. Here turn left, briefly, at a junction of paths, then right to bridge the feeder crossed on the outward leg and climb a waymarked, stepped path.

⑤ On reaching a road, almost at its end, turn right along it using a roadside footpath. Turn right at its other end, briefly, then left at a junction, going along a road that curves left short of the castle. At the road end turn right along Market Street back to the Golden Lion, where a warm welcome awaits you.

Greta Bridge
The Morritt Arms Hotel

This romantic heart of Teesdale has for centuries attracted many famous writers and artists such as Charles Dickens and JMW Turner. For here, where the rivers Greta and Tees meet, the scenery can be restful or dramatic with fields and woodland and fast flowing waters.

For years romantic Greta Bridge has inspired many well known artists and writers. In 1839 Charles Dickens stayed there whilst researching for *Nicholas Nickleby*. In the book Greta Bridge was a meeting place for his characters Nicholas Nickleby and Wackford Squeers. Towards the end of the 18th century and the beginning of the 19th century, artists such as Turner and Cotman painted Greta Bridge, the 'meeting of the waters' of the Greta and Tees rivers and other Teesdale beauty spots.

The Morritt Arms Hotel, formerly owned by the Morritt family, was bought by the present owners, Barbara and Peter, in 1994 and they have taken great delight in maintaining its historical and cultural heritage with carefully chosen antiques and original paintings. The Dickens Bar, with it famous mural painted by Jack Gilroy, and Pallatt's Bistro offer a relaxed and informal setting in which to enjoy traditional British fare and a selection of local ales. Gilroy's restaurant is reputed to be one of the finest dining experiences in the area. Its delicious food uses only the best local produce available. The day-time dining hours are from 10 am to 5.30 pm and the Morritt afternoon tea – Earl Grey and Darjeeling among others – is served between 3 pm and 5.30 pm. The freshly made sandwiches are delicious.

Telephone: 01833 627232

● **HOW TO GET THERE:** Take the A1, from north or south, to Scotch Corner then go west along the A66 for 9 miles to Greta Bridge.

● **PARKING:** There is a large car park for Morritt Arms patrons in front of the hotel.

● **LENGTH OF THE WALK:** 5 miles. Maps: OS Explorer 304 (W) and Outdoor Leisure Maps 30 (N) and 31 (E) (GR 086132).

THE WALK

(1) From the Morritt Arms, turn right along the road towards Greta Bridge, just before which cross a low wall on the right, as waymarked into a field. Edge it alongside the River Greta on the left and leave over a facing, waymarked stile in the field's left hand corner.

From here you can see the shady pool, Hell Cauldron, the subject of a Cotman painting.

Go forward, briefly, keeping to the right of a waymarked, fenced-in tree, continuing diagonally right up a hillside to meet a fence at a tangent at its top. Go left, alongside the fence, continuing beyond it, descending slightly, then contouring towards a fence that encloses a wooded bank on the left. Meet the fence end on and continue alongside it, on your left, soon to cross a facing stile.

The Scotchman's Stone, of which a painting by Cotman is in the British Museum, is below, left in the River Greta. Throughout its length

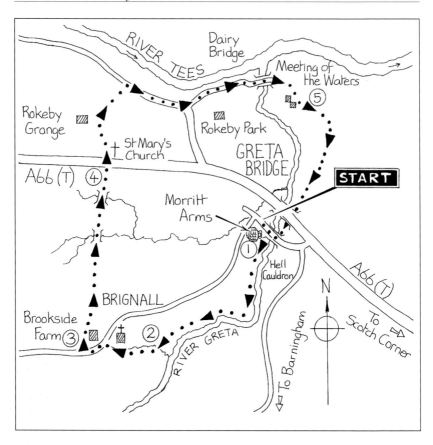

the River Greta flows along a limestone bed, much of the time confined within a steep sided wooded gorge; the Scotchman's Stone is at the downstream end.

Stay with the fence, with the Greta flowing through a deep wooded valley on your left. Most of the trees are conifers – a much favoured feeding place for coal tits. This small, almost spherical bird, seemingly without a neck and with long, spindly legs, is a glossy black with white patches on face and head.

Where the fence makes an obtuse right turn, cross a stile in it and descend a steep hillside. Cross a narrow stream and follow a contouring path that leads to a gateway in a facing wall.

Now the first of three churches along the route dedicated to Mary the Virgin is seen ahead in a walled churchyard near the river. Ruinous now, it served a medieval village, now vanished, called Brignall.

Slightly upstream of it rise Brignall Banks where the Victorian art critic John Ruskin once stood, 'looking down into the glen at twilight, the sky still full of soft rays though the sun is gone, and the Greta glances brightly in the valley, singing its even-song'.

② Once through the gateway bear left briefly and, just before a stream, turn right along a climbing path that soon bridges the stream. Continue diagonally right uphill on a clear track. From the bank top, turn right alongside a fence on your left, as waymarked. On reaching the fence corner, turn left, still alongside it, now with a ghyll on your right. Where both fence and ghyll turn left, do likewise, following a lane that soon bridges the ghyll and passes the second St Mary's church.

The lane leads through a gate to a facing minor road, Brignall Lane. Turn left along it briefly

③ Very shortly turn right into Brignall village. On reaching Brookside Farm, turn right, as waymarked, along the farm road. From its end go through a facing double gate, then diagonally left by the side of a Dutch barn. Turn right alongside it to go through a facing gate into a long field. Turn right to its corner, then left, edging the field, and continuing past a gap to go through a second one. Continue in the same direction, now with a hedge on your left soon to edge woodland on the left. When a yellow arrow on a post is reached, turn left through the narrow wood, bridging a stream. On leaving the woodland, turn right edging it soon to bridge another stream. Climb the bank ahead, following a path that leads to a waymarked post, and enter more woodland.

Descend a stepped path, cross a steam on a footbridge and climb the stepped path ahead. Skirt round the field to a stile on your right. Cross it and turn left along a fenced lane. Exit over a facing stile.

④ Cross the A66 with care and turn right briefly, then left, as waymarked, to cross the churchyard of St Mary's church number three.

Cross a facing, waymarked stile and keep straight ahead alongside a fence and line of trees on the left. Exit over a waymarked stile alongside a gate and descend the field ahead diagonally left.

Near the bottom of the field a waymarker confirms your route. Cross a stile alongside a facing gate and turn right, along a minor road. Where it turns right, go left along another minor road that soon curves right, edging the Tees to its confluence with the Greta at the Meeting of the Waters, where it turns right, briefly, then left, crossing

The 15th century Mortham Tower is said to be haunted.

the Greta on Dairy Bridge. Continue along the road, curving right towards Mortham Tower.

Mortham Tower, a 15th century peel tower, is haunted by the ghost of an aristocratic lady, said to be one of the ladies of Rokeby who was shot dead in Mortham Wood by a robber. Her blood stains the stairs of Mortham Tower.

⑤ Just before a facing gateway, turn left following a track alongside a wall and outbuildings on the right. Cross a stile alongside a facing gateway and at once turn right along a track that curves left. Cross a stile alongside a gate and keep straight ahead to just short of a Dutch barn where you turn right, as waymarked, along another track. From its end, go through a wicket and continue forward alongside first a hedge, then a wall.

Where the wall ends turn right briefly, and curve left, edging the field to exit at a stile. Descend the field ahead and, at its far end, follow an underpass below the A66. Bear left across the next field, leaving through a gap stile left of two beech trees. Turn right along the road, back to the Morritt Arms, crossing the Greta on Greta Bridge.

Greta Bridge was built in 1789, at a cost of £850 by Mr R J S Morritt. The architect was John Carr of York. The structure consists of one main, graceful, segmental arch, complete with balustraded parapets. It is 80 feet from end to end. A famous watercolour of Greta Bridge was painted by Cotman in 1810.

Low Coniscliffe
The Baydale Beck

This gentle perambulation through flat landscape is delightful and particularly suited to 'twitchers', especially during the winter months when gregarious pink-footed geese are often seen in noisy flight or feeding on the cultivated fields. Along the river bank those master fishers of infinite patience, the heron, can be seen throughout the year. These are but two of the many birds frequenting this length of the Tees and bringing thrilling spectacle to this delightful walk.

Low Coniscliffe, a neat rectangle of desirable residences, is a dormitory village set among low lying fields with its back to the River Tees, a haunt of fishermen. The Baydale Beck stands just outside the village on the A67. It is not known exactly when the Baydale Beck was built, but a building has stood on the site for the past 400 years. The original structure was of cobble stones from the nearby Tees. In its early days the inn was famous for the gangs of thieves and rogues who frequented it, especially the cut throat Cattons Gang. The robber Sir William Brown used it as his headquarters until he was tried and executed at Newcastle in 1743. It is thought that his ghost haunts the inn, although one Christopher Simpson was murdered there in 1624, so the ghost may be his. During the latter part of his career, Dick Turpin was supposed to have used the Baydale Beck, staying in a room with five doors for ease of escape. By 1824 the inn had become so notorious that the then landlord sold the property for eight shillings.

In 1871, the inn was purchased by John Theakston, (1829-1881) a master butcher of Northgate, Darlington, at an auction in Darlington's King's Head Hotel. The Baydale Beck became a regular eating place for young Darlington folk who enjoyed the Scotch oat cakes and whisky served by the landlady, Mrs Nesbitt.

Today it is renowned as an ideal venue for families seeking good food and drink. There is a family room, a beer garden and a play area for children. Well behaved dogs are welcome in the beer garden, where water bowls are provided if requested, but not in the pub itself.

The Baydale Beck menu offers sumptuous food with mouth-watering starters like soup of the day with warm baguette, Greek salad and Dublin prawns. Main courses include such gastronomic delights as breast of local duck marinated and cooked with oriental spices, 8oz steaks, peppered beef stroganoff and Scottish salmon. There is a children's and an OAP's menu and with the home made meals you buy one, get one half price, from Monday to Saturday 12 noon to 2 pm and 6 pm to 9 pm, and Sunday from 12 noon to 3 pm and 6 pm to 8.30 pm.

The log fires in this children-friendly hostelry create a cosy atmosphere in which to indulge in beers like cask Magnet, Electric Magnet and Abbott's, a guest ale that was so popular it is now always available. The guest ales are changed weekly. Fosters, Kronenbourg, Carling and Stella lagers are always available and there is a large selection of red and white wines.

Telephone: 01325 469637

- **HOW TO GET THERE:** The Baydale Beck can be found on the right hand side of the A67 within 100 yards of leaving Darlington westwards.
- **PARKING:** There is a large car park to the rear of the inn.
- **LENGTH OF THE WALK:** 3 miles: Maps: OS Explorer 304 (W) and 304 (E) (GR 254141).

THE WALK

At the walk's outset, before the A67 is crossed, a detour left for 300 yards will take you to Northumberland Water's largest and latest water treatment plant. It cost £13 million to build, and is open to the public from time to time.

① From the pub cross the A67 and climb a facing stile into a field, directed by a footpath sign. Go diagonally right across the field, leaving through a facing waymarked stile at its right-hand corner. Edge the field ahead, close to a hedge on the right, leaving through a facing stile. Continue along a narrow lane into Low Coniscliffe. At the lane end, turn left, through the village. In a short distance turn left, directed by a Teesdale Way signpost, and go between buildings towards the river.

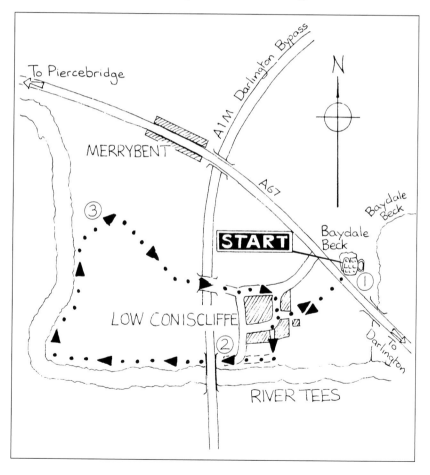

Turn right along a track, crossing a stile, and continuing, close to the river on your left. At the end of the track cross a facing step stile and continue straight head along an unclassified road, going through a kissing gate alongside a gate, soon to reach the bridge carrying the A1(M), Darlington bypass over the Tees.

The ancient ford that crosses the river at this point links Low Coniscliffe on the north bank to another village, Cleasby.

② Go under the bridge and follow a clear riverside path upstream. The Tees is close to your left and flat, agricultural land is to your right. In about 3/4 mile, another clear path leaves the river at right angles, but do not take it. Instead, continue along the riverside path, which soon turns sharp right with the river.

Cross a facing stile and continue upstream, edging the field ahead, only now with a flood barrier between you and the river. At the end of the field, ignore a facing waymarked stile which leads to the flat top of the barrier and keep on a clear path that follows the flood barrier's foot. The path along the top of the flood barrier is very overgrown.

In a short distance the path alongside the barrier's foot slices through it and continues, clear as can be, through narrow woodland alongside the river.

③ At a fork in the path, go right, up a bank, away from the river, to join a very clear field track which leaves the river at right angles. Follow it across the flat field, curving right in the middle of it towards the A1(M) seen ahead.

Merrybent, a dormitory village, spreads along a ridge over on the left: two rows of prosperous houses with the A67 between them.

As the track curves right, a public footpath sign on a post confirms your route. Stay on the track, which reaches and bridges the motorway then descends to a large gate with a wicket alongside it. Go through the wicket and immediately turn left along a tarmac road, edging Low Coniscliffe on the right. At the road end, turn right, into the village, briefly. Where the road curves right, turn left at a footpath sign and retrace your steps to the Baydale Beck inn.

Neasham

The Fox and Hounds

This is an easy stroll through a delightfully varied landscape. The balance of arable fields and woodland is good and the views are surprisingly expansive for so little effort. The climbs are gently, the hedgerows awash with flowers for much of the year and fallow deer are frequently seen.

Low-lying Neasham hides behind a pleasant, grass-covered flood barrier, its gardens, in season, a blaze of colour. Like the New English Hymnal, it is a happy blend of ancient and modern. At its western end Neasham Abbey, an early 19th century villa, stands near the site of a Benedictine nunnery, founded around 1156 and dedicated to the Virgin Mary. The rectangular shelter at the foot of Neasham Hill, to the east of the village, was originally a pump house, built in 1879.

A headless apparition is said to haunt the road between Neasham and Hurworth, the next village upsteam. But if it is spirits you are seeking, you could do better to look no further than the Fox and Hounds, smack in the middle of Neasham. As its name implies, this is a very rustic pub with oak beams, rural prints and shelves awash with pewter tankards and plates, all of which contribute to a rich, country atmosphere.

Steaks of locally bought beef are a speciality. They are hung for a minimum of 14 days with the surplus fat removed, ready to be grilled to your liking. Fish courses include large cod in crispy batter, haddock fillets and salmon steak. Main meals, be it steak and kidney pie, ham and mushroom tagliatelle or lasagne – and there are many more – are all served with a choice of salad, vegetables, boiled potatoes, chips or rice. There are vegetarian dishes, omelettes, fresh cut sandwiches and attractive meals for children. Ingredients are locally bought where possible, and the menu is changed every two weeks. Food is served every day between 12 noon and 2 pm and from 6.30 pm (7 pm Sundays) to 9 pm. Thirst quenchers include a rotating selection of cask ales including Exmoor Wild Cat and other similar brews. Guinness, various lagers and soft drinks are also available. Dogs on a lead are welcome in the garden, but not in the pub itself.

Telephone: 01325 720350

- **HOW TO GET THERE:** Neasham lies 2 miles south of Darlington. From the A66 outer ring road, driving eastwards, turn right at the first roundabout after bridging the main railway line, along Neasham Road. At its end, turn left into Neasham. The Fox and Hounds is soon reached on the right.
- **PARKING:** Ample parking is available for patrons in the pub car park.
- **LENGTH OF THE WALK:** 3½ miles: Map: OS Explorer 304 (E) (GR 325101).

THE WALK

(1) From the Fox and Hounds go diagonally right across the road and bear left along metalled New Lane as waymarked. On leaving Neasham, the lane becomes an unsurfaced track that cuts through arable land, bridges a stream and continues to Neasham Springs Farm on rising ground. The track is mostly unenclosed with just the odd tree alongside it at irregular intervals. It is easy to follow.

On approaching Neasham Springs Farm, a blue arrow on a post confirms your route as the track climbs and turns left in front of the farmhouse. It then turns right between the farmhouse and farm buildings and continues straight ahead edging a field close to a hedge on the left. Soon the hedge becomes a fence and its first post carries a waymarker. Simply follow the track which continues along a waymarked lane.

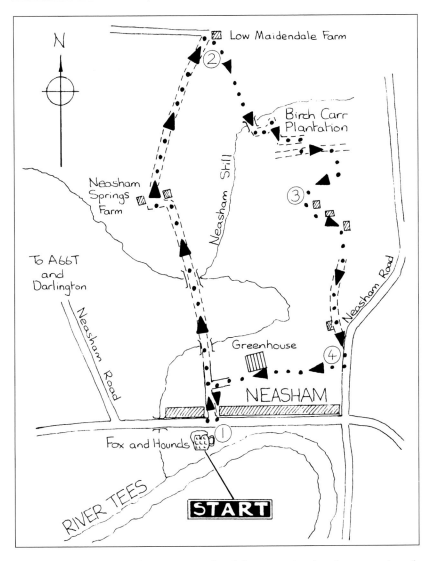

As progress is made, Low Maidendale Farm is clearly seen ahead, slightly to the right. The lane curves right, towards the farmhouse.

(2) Just short of it, where a farm road is met at a tangent on the left, turn right, over a stile in the fence on the right. Go diagonally left across a paddock, directed by a yellow arrow and exit through a waymarked wicket in a facing fence. Skirt the field ahead close to a hedge on the right, leaving over a footbridge across Neasham Still at the right hand

corner of a facing fence. Bear left along a climbing path through shrub. The path soon turns sharp left and crosses a ditch, beyond which it turns right, briefly, to a waymarked stile in a facing fence. Cross the stile and keep straight ahead, guided by a yellow arrow, contouring the bank parallel to a fence on your left and following a path. Go through a facing waymarked gate and immediately turn right, briefly, edging a pasture to cross a stile alongside a facing right hand corner gate.

Keep straight ahead, following a path along the bottom of a wooded slope on your left. It soon curves left, through shallow Birch Carr Plantation, leaving over a waymarked stile to the left of a facing gate into a field. Continue forward, edging a short fence on the right. At its end, cross a ditch on your right, on a plank bridge, as waymarked, and climb a sloping field alongside a fence on your right. On reaching a facing hedge, turn left, alongside it. Turn right through a gate and edge the next field close to a hedge on the left, following a clear track with Cold Comfort Farm seen ahead.

③ Leave the field over a waymarked stile alongside a gate in the left hand corner of a facing fence. From here go diagonally right, descending and aiming for the right hand corner of the fence surrounding Cold Comfort Farm, continuing beyond the corner in the same direction to cross a waymarked stile in a facing fence. Continue alongside a fence on your left and a little way beyond it to cross a facing waymarked stile. Now go diagonally right, as waymarked, and where the land falls away steeply, keep to the left of a fenced wooded area containing a shelter to leave the field over a facing stile in a kink in a facing fence. Immediately turn right, as waymarked, crossing a ditch on a plank bridge, and follow a clear path along the foot of a wooded bank on your left.

Soon a bungalow is passed on the right. Continue along its approach road to join Neasham road at a tangent. Keep straight ahead, along a roadside footpath, for 100 yards, where you turn right, through a gap stile at the footpath sign.

④ Edge the field ahead along the flat top of an embankment. Turn right at a facing fence, leaving the embankment, and bear left along a clear path soon to pass greenhouses on the right. Go through a double gate and along a short, tarmac road to a T-junction, where the lane used on the outward leg is regained. Turn left, along it, briefly, retracing your steps to the Fox and Hounds.

Middleton-One-Row
The Devonport Hotel

A panoramic view across the river Tees to the purple hills of distant Cleveland brings an excitement to this walk which is maintained throughout. For the first 1¹/₂ miles the route threads a thickly-wooded scarp, along which, every spring, an explosion of wildflowers – primroses, violets, celandines, wood anemones and wild garlic – colours the undergrowth. The walk continues across lush fields and a golf course, and is mostly along paths and field tracks, always on clearly defined rights of way.

Middleton-One-Row is magnificently sited high on an embankment where the Tees, in its middle reaches, performs one of its superb bends. The river is the county boundary here and Middleton-One-Row, on the elevated Durham bank, enjoys a sweeping view across a low-lying part of rural Yorkshire.

The Devonport Hotel is in the heart of the village, overlooking picturesque countryside that extends to the Cleveland Hills. Formerly a row of cottages, the building is at least 300 years old. It is a beautiful country inn that exudes great charm. It has 16 en suite rooms available for residents, two restaurants, a lounge bar and a 'locals' bar, all full of character; and the food is a gourmet's dream. Whatever your fancy, be it fillets of Dover sole wrapped in smoked salmon with lobster sauce, oxtails in red wine and onions, oriental dishes or Desperate Dan's real ale pie, the Devonport Hotel is competent to provide it. To complement your meal there is a selection of over 80 wines from around the world, while, in the bars, real ales from Theakston and Marston are supplemented by regular guest beers.

Telephone: 01325 332255

- **HOW TO GET THERE:** Middleton-One-Row lies some 3 miles south-east of Darlington. Take the A67 eastwards from Darlington to Middleton-St-George, turn right at a junction in the village and follow an unclassified road southwards for just over 1/2 mile, to where it turns sharp left into Middleton-One-Row. The Devonport Hotel is midway along the village, on the left.
- **PARKING:** Patrons can park on the hotel's forecourt.
- **LENGTH OF THE WALK:** 4 1/2 miles. Map: OS Explorer 304 (E) (GR 153123).

THE WALK

① From the Devonport Hotel go diagonally right across the road to join the Teesdale Way at a footpath sign. Turn right along another path, cross a waymarked stile and continue upstream into Dinsdale Wood. The path edges the river most pleasantly, soon to reach a surfaced road, known as Pountey's Lane from the Roman *pons tesie*, the approach road to a bridge, long gone, which crossed the river close to where the road turns right.

Continue along this road, parallel to the Tees, soon to reach a large house, where the road ends. This is Dinsdale Spa.

In 1789, men looking for coal sources along the banks of the Tees broke through a layer of rock and released a stream of sulphurous water. At that time mineral springs were thought to be a cure for all

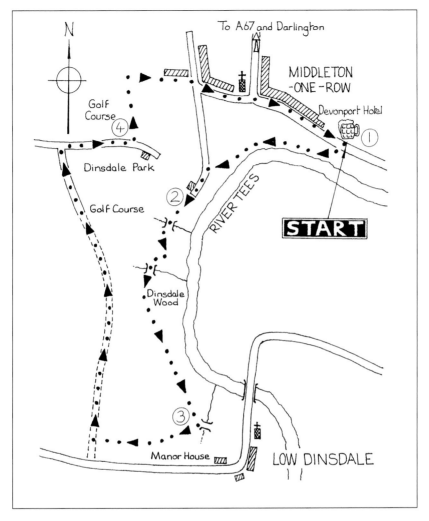

ailments, so Dinsdale Spa came into being. Although never as popular as Buxton or Bath, Dinsdale Spa was thought by the Stockton and Darlington Railway Company to have potential and they built Dinsdale station to accommodate the anticipated passenger traffic.

② Pass the house, cross a facing stile and continue through woodland along a contouring path. Soon a feeder stream is crossed on a footbridge and, a little beyond it, the path climbs quite steeply, then levels for a short distance before descending, curving right, then left, to bridge another stream.

77

As the path meanders pleasantly through the greenery, the Tees is glimpsed below, on the left. This stretch of water is often frequented by herons.

Leave the wood over a facing step stile into a field. Cross this on a faint green path, which passes to the right of a telegraph pole, beyond which you bear left to reach a small, concrete bridge over a ditch.

From here Low Dinsdale, a working village with lots of character, spreads itself between protective trees. Prominent is its pink sandstone church, surrounded by copper beeches. The oldest building in the village, Dinsdale Manor House, dates mainly from the Tudor period but contains some 13th century masonry.

③ Do not cross the concrete bridge. Instead, turn right and aim for the second of two telegraph poles, seen ahead immediately behind a facing fence. Cross the stile in the fence here and immediately turn right along a path that edges the field on rising ground close to the hedge on your right. Exit over a waymarked stile in the right hand corner of a facing fence. Turn right along a broad, clear track, edging the field close to a hedge on your right, soon to go alongside Dinsdale Wood on the right, beyond which it skirts a golf course, also on the right, before going straight into it.

Keep straight ahead, still on the broad track, ignoring an arrow pointing right along a narrow track. Exit the golf course onto a minor road and turn right along it, directed by a footpath sign. The road is very quiet and it soon reaches a large building on the right, Dinsdale Park, once a nursing home.

④ At this point where the road curves right, turn left, as waymarked, into another area of the golf course. Cross it, diagonally right, directed by a yellow arrow, soon to pass, on your left, a deep pond and a small copse of oak trees. A little further on there is a seat, should you fancy a sit down.

Leave the golf course through a gap stile in the left hand corner of a facing fence. Immediately turn right along a path, close to a fence on your right. Leave the field through a facing gap stile and keep straight ahead, directed by a yellow arrow, still keeping close to the fence on the right. As you follow the path, a yellow arrow on a post confirms your route. Leave the field over a facing stile to the left of a gate.

Keep straight ahead, now along a roadside footpath between dwellings. Soon St Lawrence's church is passed on the left, at the road's end. Go straight ahead, into Middleton-One-Row, soon to reach the Devonport Hotel.

Newton Under Roseberry
The King's Head

A giant Saxon king called Wada, or Wade, had a tall wife called Bell. She had a cow and to milk it she had to tramp across the moors. So Wade built her a road called Wade's Causeway. Any spare earth he dug up, he used to form Blakey Topping and Roseberry Topping. Such is the legend behind this outstanding walk, which climbs through wonderful country to the summit of Teesside's best known landmark. The descent maintains all the thrill of the climb, bringing a glorious dream to brilliant reality.

Roseberry Topping has shrunk. It once stood 1,067 feet above sea level, but is now reduced in height because of mining. Even so, this craggy outlier of the Tabular Hills towers so dramatically above the surrounding landscape that it is known as Yorkshire's Matterhorn. The word 'topping' is derived from the Danish 'toppen', meaning summit, but the peak was originally called Odin's Berg and the name had many variations. It was not known as Roseberry Topping until after 1600.

The distinctive shape of the peak has been formed due to the combination of surface erosion and underground mining. It has an oolithic cap which protects the underlying lias. Roseberry Topping sometimes wears another kind of cap, as this couplet shows:

When Roseberry Topping wears a cap,
Cleveland then beware a clap.

The King's Head has an atmosphere that positively reeks of romance. Built in 1796, it was originally a manor house. It has low ceilings and oak beams. Its roof is supported on trees as they were hewn with the bark still on them. Overshadowed by Roseberry Topping, its chief claim to fame once lay in a particular brew of draught porter, which was renowned for miles around.

Once an annual event of great jollification, the Trinityside Fair, was held on Roseberry Topping and the King's Head was a meeting place for those who thronged to it.

Today, dining at the King's Head is like banqueting at a royal feast. From the Royal Grill come delectable morsels like de-fatted sirloin steaks, and the King's Saucy Specials include succulent Solway specials and other delicious dishes. Chilled draught wines by the glass or carafe are always available and draught real ale goes down a treat.

The hotel has wheelchair access and toilets for the disabled.

Telephone: 01642 722318

● **HOW TO GET THERE:** From the west end of Guisborough take the A173, the Great Ayton road, to reach Newton-Under-Roseberry in 2¹/₂ miles. The King's Head is on the left midway through the village.

● **PARKING:** A car park, for patrons, with security camera surveillance at the rear of the hotel can hold 80 vehicles.

● **LENGTH OF THE WALK:** 2¹/₂ miles. Map: Outdoor Leisure 26 (N) (GR 571129).

THE WALK

① From the King's Head turn left along a roadside footpath and, just past the last building on the left, turn left, directed by a footpath sign, into Roseberry Lane. In a short distance go through a facing gate. Continue along the lane towards the bottom of Roseberry Topping. On approaching the entrance to Newton Wood, turn left, with the lane contouring and going through a facing gate. Keep straight ahead, climbing gently, going left at a fork, soon to meet a green path at a tangent. Continue along it in the same direction, still contouring, now through bracken.

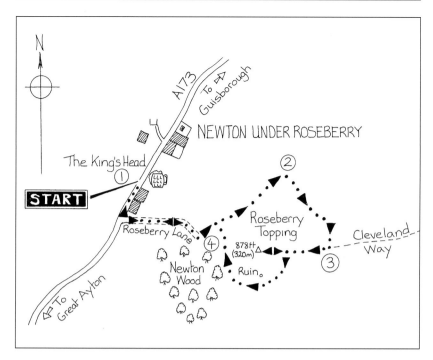

Meadow Brown butterflies are found in great numbers around here, flitting merrily about these bracken-clad slopes during the summer months. The male has a small black spot on the back wing: the female hasn't.

② In a short distance the path curves right and climbs quite steeply, soon to reach at a tangent another path coming from the right. Continue left along it, crossing the head of a little valley, then, where the path splits, take the right hand, climbing one.

③ On reaching a clear path at right angles, turn right along it and climb to the summit of Roseberry Topping.

There was once a hermitage near the top of Roseberry Topping, now gone, and there was also a well there. The summit was also once used as a site for a beacon.

In a play performed in London in the 18th century, a character declared that Roseberry Topping was 'Half a mile high and as cold as ice at the top'.

A trig point marks the summit of Roseberry Topping at 878 feet. It is a popular spot and from all-round the views are breathtaking and it is well worth the energy expended in getting there. To westwards, in the near distance, is Great Ayton where Captain James Cook went to school. As a boy he lived at Aireyholme Farm, near the foot of Roseberry Topping, where his father worked and where Cook himself worked for two years. There is an imposing monument to Captain Cook on Easby Moor, to the south east of Great Ayton.

From the trig point retrace your steps for about 100 yards passing the first path descending on your right. Turn right at the second one, which curves right as it descends to meet the first track, midway down the slope. (It is quite in order to use the first path but the second one has a firmer surface.)

From the meeting of paths continue descending through bracken, bearing right along a clear path, soon to reach a fence. Turn right alongside it on your left, contouring at first, then descending to go through a gate in the left hand corner of a facing fence. Once through the gate go forward, keeping to the right of a stone-built shooting box. It was built by Commodore Wilson of Ayton Hall as a lunch-time shelter for shooters in inclement weather.

Descend a bank and, as the ground becomes less steep, bear right, to cross a stile in the left hand corner of a facing fence, ignoring the stile seen ahead as you descend the bank. Ignore the stile on the left immediately past the one just crossed and keep straight ahead, outside Newton Wood and a little away from it, following a path through bracken.

④ On reaching a broad path at right angles, turn left downhill. Go through a facing gate and continue downwards, using a stepped path, which keeps above the wood and curves right. Ignore any side paths into the wood, soon to descend quite steeply to cross a facing path, then continue downhill a little further to go through a facing gate. Immediately turn left, go through another gate and retrace your steps along Roseberry Lane and from there back to The King's Head.

Lingdale
The Lingdale Tavern

A beautiful, steep-sided, wooded valley is crossed twice on this most pleasing walk through fields and along narrow country lanes.

Lingdale village was built to house employees of the Lingdale Iron Stone Mine, which operated from 1878 until 1962, and the Lingdale Tavern (around 120 years old) was once a hotel used by personnel associated with the mine.

The restaurant floor is one of the best sprung dance floors in the Teesside area. Most of the local wedding receptions and dances were held there and an excellent sword dancing team performed there regularly.

Tempting bar meals are served daily both at lunchtimes and in the evenings with a choice of starters, main courses diverse enough to satisfy all tastes and a rich assortment of sweets. There is always a children's choice and a daily special. The carvery in the Woodlands

Restaurant offers a choice of two roasts from which to help yourself, vegetable dishes are available and the chef is there to help you decide, no easy task when you are spoiled for choice. A traditional Sunday lunch is also served in the family room.

Drinking hours are 11.30 am to 4 pm and 7 pm to 11 pm Monday to Thursday; 11.30 am to 11 pm Friday and Saturday; and from 12 noon to 3 pm and 7 pm to 10.30 pm on Sundays. The one real ale always available is John Smith's best bitter and Woodpecker and Strongbow ciders are on draught.

A previous landlord had a black dog which used to lay in the bar. Its ghost still does, according to a great many locals, some of whom, to their horror, have bent to stroke it only to find nothing there.

The Lingdale Tavern is a free house full of character. It is very friendly, the beer is good and the fare is even better.

Telephone: 01287 650267

- **HOW TO GET THERE:** Take the A171 eastwards from Guisborough for 5 miles and just before it edges Lockwood Beck restaurant turn left along Stanghow Road for 1½ miles to reach Lingdale. The Lingdale Tavern occupies a corner site on the left at the village crossroads.
- **PARKING:** The Lingdale Tavern car park, on the west side of the pub.
- **LENGTH OF THE WALK:** 3½ miles. Maps: OS Explorer 306 and Outdoor Leisure 26 (N) (GR 675163).

THE WALK

(1) From Lingdale Tavern cross Stanghow Road and continue along a side road met end on, using a roadside footpath. On reaching a roundabout, turn right and go through a gate and skirt round a playing field close to a hedge on the left. From its left hand corner continue along a clear path to a facing stile, which you cross, ignoring the one on the right. Follow the path ahead edging dwellings on the left and exit through a kissing gate in the fence on the left. Immediately turn right to continue across a rough pasture, bearing slightly left. At first you are on rising ground, then you descend into a hollow to go between a pair of stone gateposts, beyond which take a track uphill to go through a facing kissing gate at a footpath sign.

(2) Cross an unclassified road, diagonally right, go through another kissing gate at a huge public right of way sign and follow a lane, walled on the left, fenced on the right. Conical Freebrough Hill, a local landmark, is now seen straight ahead.

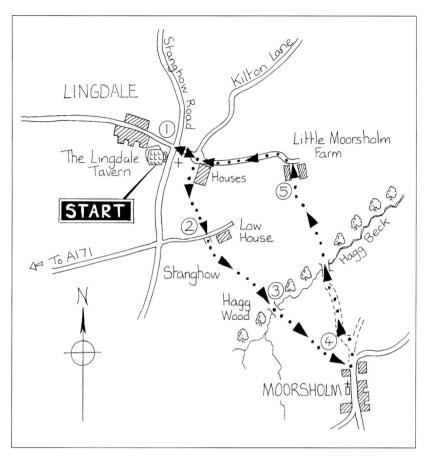

Leave this short lane through a facing kissing gate and cross a farm road as it curves left across your line of walk. Go through a kissing gate at another public right of way sign. Edge the field ahead along a fenced lane and at its end turn left, through a waymarked kissing gate. Continue diagonally right to the valley bottom, directed by a yellow arrow at the end of a fence. On reaching the fence, continue alongside it on the right through a rather boggy area. Continue alongside a fence which then becomes a wall. The field is a long one and as you approach its far end, a facing waymarked stile can be seen some 30 yards left of the field's right hand corner.

Cross this stile into woodland and follow a path between trees, directed by a yellow arrow, bearing right, then curving left and becoming stepped as it descends bush and bracken clad banks, richly adorned with brambles and a variety of shade loving plants and flowers.

③ In the valley bottom the path crosses Hagg Beck on a footbridge and climbs up the valley side to the wood's edge.

A feature of this part of Teesside is its narrow, steep sided valleys of which this is one.

Exit over a waymarked stile in the right hand corner of a fence on your left and edge the field ahead close to the fence on your right. At the end of the field cross a waymarked stile in the right hand corner of a facing fence. Go diagonally right across the ridged field ahead, leaving over a stile in the fence on the left at a telegraph pole near the field's corner.

Cross the field ahead on rising ground, go over a facing, waymarked stile into a passage between dwellings and, at its end guided by a footpath sign descend a flight of four steps onto the road at the north end of Moorsholm village.

Shades of *Wind In The Willows*: the pub across the road is Toad Hall.

Turn left, along the road, and where it curves right, leaving the village, turn left at a footpath sign, along a lane.

④ In a short distance, the lane curves right. Keep straight ahead, as waymarked, along a short, concrete approach to a field. From here, the North Sea is seen straight ahead.

At the end of the field's approach, bear left along a narrow, hedged lane that is flagged for a short distance. After almost ½ mile, the lane ends and the clear path continues through Hagg Wood, descending to re-cross Hagg Beck on a footbridge, downstream of the first crossing. Continue along the clear path, which bears right and climbs steadily for some distance parallel to Hagg Beck on the right. Near the rim of the valley, the path curves away from the beck. It leaves the wood along a hedged lane. From the lane end keep straight ahead, close to a hedge on the left, edging arable land.

⑤ On reaching a farm road coming from the left continue along it. In a short distance turn right towards Little Moorsholm Farm. Just before the farm buildings turn left along the path, between outbuildings, to join a minor road at its end. Follow the road to its other end, and turn left, briefly, to the roundabout, from where you retrace your steps to The Lingdale Tavern.

Brotton
The Queens Arms

The descent from Brotton to the coast through pleasant fields to join and share for a little while the renowned Cleveland Way, offers fine seascapes. The cliffs are rich in flowers and sea birds and the panoramic views from Warsett Hill and the contouring track above Hunley Hall Golf Club ensure that the interest never flags.

Danish Brotton is recorded in the Domesday Survey of 1086 as Broctune or Brotune. It stood on high ground in the middle of a great forest where wolves, wild boar and deer roamed. From this vantage point, mile after mile of lovely green hills and valleys could be seen, with a broad sweep of sea to the east. The village expanded in 1861 when ironstone was discovered in these hills. The village green has been built over, but today's irregular layout shows where it was situated long ago.

The Queens Arms occupies a prominent hilltop across the road from Brotton church, as it has done for over 300 years. The open space behind the pub is known as the blood tub because it was there that, for decades, bare-knuckle boxing contests were regularly held.

The Queens Arms exudes warmth: its atmosphere is very friendly and it is highly recommended for the superlative quality of the meals served there: it is the best food for miles around. The succulent roasts come complete with all the trimmings and the vegetables are always fresh. Cajun chicken and home made steak pies are very popular as is the remainder of the exciting menu.

There is a good selection of drinks available, including John Smith's Magnet, cider and Guinness.

Telephone: 01287 679512

- **HOW TO GET THERE:** Brotton is a small town 2 miles south east of Saltburn on the A174. The Queens Arms is on the right of this road on the crest of a hill towards the eastern end of the town.
- **PARKING:** A car park for patrons at the rear of the Queens Arms.
- **LENGTH OF THE WALK:** 4 miles. Maps: OS Explorer 306 and Outdoor Leisure 26 (N) (GR 692198).

THE WALK

① From the Queens Arms turn right along a roadside footpath, keeping straight ahead at a crossroad.

② A few yards past the last building on the left, turn left at a footpath. Go along a path that bears right, descending and becoming

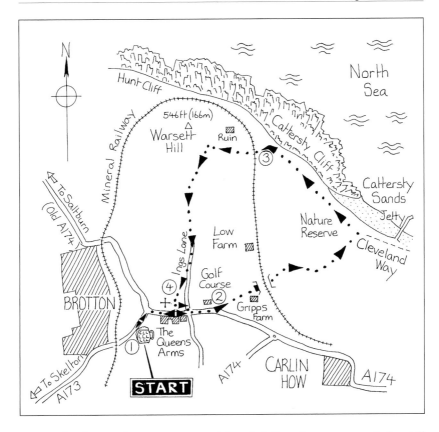

stepped. The path soon turns right, briefly, then curves left, still descending, soon to pass Gripps Farm on the right, beyond which it becomes much wider and very clear. In a short distance it goes under a railway bridge.

Hunley Hall golf course is clearly seen, a field away, on the left and ahead there is a large expanse of sea, choppy and with long, white breakers when we were there. Coasters were cutting through the blue water on regular coastal runs.

The broad path continues beyond the bridge, taking a very clear route through more arable land, alongside a hedge on the left for a short distance. Go through a facing gate and follow a track that soon curves right towards a facing fence. Turn left along a fenced lane, the fence on your left.

You are now edging Cattersty Gill Nature Reserve on your left. Before restoration in 1975, this flower meadow was a slag heap for a nearby steel works. Luckily most of the shrub-filled coastal site survived and now provides an important, and very welcome, resting and refuelling stop for winter migrant birds. The salt winds help maintain the conditions for the grasses here but the strong winds on the cliff top make shrub growth difficult.

Ignore a waymarked wicket in the fence and stay alongside it until a waymarked gate is reached. Go through the gate and head along a broad, green track that edges the cliff top.

The cliff is fairly low at this point and the Cleveland Way runs along its foot. In a short distance the Cleveland Way climbs the boulder slag and the two walks become one, climbing steadily as the cliff gains a height of over 800 feet.

Ignore any fence stiles and stay on the clear cliff-top path, which soon turns inland, briefly, to skirt an inlet. Here ignore two more closely sited stiles at the head of the inlet and stay on the cliff-top path.

③ When a ruin can be seen ahead, look for a Countryside Commission stile in the fence on your left, cross it and follow a clear green path that climbs the field ahead at right angles to the cliff.

You are now on Warsett Hill, which was purchased by the National Trust in 1991 with the help of local donations and the Enterprise Neptune appeal. The ruin, which is now to your right as you cross the field, the only building on the site, was a fan house used to ventilate an iron stone mine from 1872 until 1906.

The coastline around here has some of the most spectacular cliffs in England, including flat-topped Hunt Cliff promontory, which drops precipitously below Warsett Hill, 546 feet above the sea.

Leave the field over a ladder stile and cross the railway line, still in use, with great care, exiting over a step stile. Climb the field ahead aiming for a clearly seen stile in a facing fence some 150 yards left of a gate. Once through the stile, continue up the side of Warsett Hill. On approaching another facing fence at its top, bear left to a waymarked stile alongside a gateway in the fence on the left. Cross it and follow the clear track ahead.

Behind and to eastwards the sea spreads to the horizon, to westwards Roseberry Topping, and Guisborough Woods can be seen and ahead is Brotton. There are no hedges on the right-hand higher side of the track, and behind the one on the left is Hunley Hall golf course.

④ At its end the track gets a concrete surface and turns left alongside Hunley Hall club house, then turns right to meet a tarmac road, Ings

The coast looking towards the jetty at Skinningrove.

Lane which climbs to go round a sharp corner. Short of this bend, turn left along a clear track, which curves right between a plantation on the left and dwellings. On reaching a passage on the right, between houses, turn right along it. At its end, turn left along a roadside footpath. In a few yards turn left along Ings Lane using a roadside footpath. On reaching a crossroad turn right and retrace your steps to the Queens Arms.

Saltburn
The Ship

Some 250 years ago the safest and most profitable policy for visitors to Saltburn was to ask no questions. The wife of a visitor, staying at the Ship, was given this sound advice:

If you wake at midnight and hear the horses' feet,
Don't go drawing back the blind or looking in the street.
Them that asks no questions isn't told a lie,
Watch the wall, my darling, while the gentlemen go by.

Saltburn occupies an elevated position overlooking Saltburn Sands. It is a genteel holiday resort much frequented by those who prefer a more sedate ambience to the 'kiss me quick' ostentation of nearby Redcar. It stands at the northern end of the Heritage Coast a 36-miles long stretch of coastline of outstanding natural beauty, wildlife and historic interest For many centuries Saltburn was deeply involved with the lucrative business of smuggling. When this trade peaked in the mid-17th century, Saltburn's entire population was involved. The 'king of the smugglers' at Saltburn was John Andrew, licensee of the Ship and, along with Tom King of Kirkleatham, he owned a fast cutter the *Morgan Rattler*. Whenever news spread that 'Andrew's cow has calved,' helpers knew that the cutter lay off Saltburn with a cargo to unload.

A flagstone in the stall of a horsebox at the Ship was the entrance to an underground passage where cargos were stored. Gentry and clergy helped distribute the goods and John Andrew became a gentleman on the vast profits. When finally caught he was fined £100,000, which he could not pay. He was imprisoned in York Castle and such was his influence that he was released after only two years.

Both inside and out the Ship has a 19th century look about it. Beautiful dark, shipboard planking lines most walls and part of the ceiling, and marine memorabilia and evocative seascapes adorn the saloon.

The restaurant is spacious, and there is more than a hint of the sea about the large menu, which includes fresh crab in season, Atlantic prawns, deep fried codling, scampi, cod provençale and breaded lemon sole. Meat dishes such as topside of beef, sirloin and rump steak, rack of ribs, Cumberland sausage and home-cooked ham all have the full trimmings treatment. There is regular chilli, chilli mac and house curry. Vegetarian dishes like mushroom bake are ever popular; and to wash everything down there is fresh brewed tea, Kenco percolated coffee, hot chocolate and a choice of liqueurs.

The restaurant hours are 12 noon to 2.30 pm and 6 pm to 11 pm Monday to Friday and all day Saturday and Sunday.

Telephone: 01287 622361

- **HOW TO GET THERE:** The A174, eastwards from Middlesbrough goes through Saltburn. Where it descends steeply to sea level to cross Skelton Beck before climbing towards Brotton, it passes the Ship on the left at the foot of the hill.
- **PARKING:** There are car parks for patrons in front and to the rear of the Ship.
- **LENGTH OF THE WALK:** 4$\frac{1}{2}$ miles. Maps: Explorer 306 and Outdoor Leisure 26 (N) (GR 668216).

THE WALK

(1) From the Ship turn left and, just past the car park, turn left along a steeply climbing stepped path, signposted to Hunt Cliff Nature Reserve.

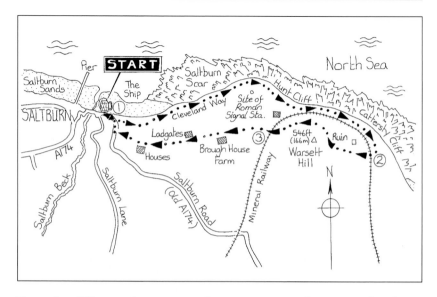

From the cliff top, where a carved stone outcrop informs you that this is the Cleveland Coast, go forward, edging the cliff top along a gently rising path from which the coastal views are excellent.

Here we overlooked a couple of oyster catchers on the sand at the foot of the cliff while, still below us, several gulls rode the thermals.

The clear path continues, going through a gap in a facing fence and continuing along the cliff top. Soon the site of a Roman signal station, Hunt Cliff, is passed. It was built to warn of seaborne raiders. By 1911 more than half had eroded away. The remainder was then excavated.

The cliff, hereabouts, is a veritable kittiwake city. Kittiwakes live out at sea feeding on squid, shrimps and molluscs. They only come ashore to breed. The nest made of moss, sea weed and other plants, is held together with a generous supply of droppings, and is built on a rocky ledge. The grass around here is rich in wild flowers and insects. Landslip disturbance is constantly providing a seed bed and a variety of conditions in which new plants can grow. It is renowned for uncommon plants like the fragrant orchid, carline thistle and dyers greenweed, which is used to make yellow dye.

The simple 'pheet' of the rock pipit is frequently heard along here. But today we have harsher cries of screeching gulls.

The path continues to climb steadily but gently and the views are beautiful. Soon a National Trust sign tells you that you have reached Warsett Hill. The further you walk along the cliff top the more exciting

A modern sculpture near Hunt Cliff.

it becomes. The path is green and clear and a joy to walk along. Below the cliff, sand has given way to rock.

On approaching Warsett Hill cross the stile to the left of the wicket in a facing fence.

The path briefly edges a railway on the right, and then forks: take either route because they both join a little further on. The left fork is the broader of the two and from it a path leads to a viewing seat where there are two metal sculptures with local themes.

② A little beyond where the paths rejoin, almost at once turn right, over a stile in the fence met end on, close to a National Trust, Warsett Hill sign.

Cross the field ahead diagonally left and edge around some rough ground, passing the air shaft building on the right. On reaching a step stile on the right, cross it and go over the railway which is single track but still in use, so care is needed. Exit over another stile into a field. Cross this, bearing slightly right on rising ground, and leaving the field through a gate in a facing fence.

Continue in the same direction following an undefined route, soon to turn right at a junction of paths to a facing fence. Cross a stile to the right of a gate and keep straight ahead on a clear path, which soon descends gently, continuing towards a facing fence. Cross a stile to the

One of the many marvellous views to be seen on this walk.

left of a gate fence, and keep ahead still on a clear path. When about midway across the field go diagonally right along a clear path to exit over a stile in a facing fence, beyond which go straight ahead, still on a clear path, across the next field. Once over another stile cross the railway line.

③ Exit over another stile and skirt round the field ahead, close to a fence on the left. Cross a facing left hand corner stile and again skirt round the next field alongside a fence on the left on a broad track. Where the track turns left beyond a cottage near Brough House Farm on the left, turn right along another broad track which immediately turns left directed by a 'Saltburn' stile, edging the left hand side of a field.

Ahead lies Saltburn with a church tower rising from its middle.

Just past Ladgates Farm, where the track splits, take the right fork, which goes straight ahead along a lane. At the lane end, go through a facing gate and down the middle of the next field, still on the clear track, which curves right. Ignore a path on the left. Stay on the track, passing to the right of some houses. Continue along a short, green lane, guided by a yellow arrow. Exit through a kissing gate onto the Cleveland Way on the cliff top. Turn left along the path and retrace your steps to the Ship.

'Ar, Jim, lad, time to splice the main brace.'